Library of Congress Cataloging-in-Publication Data

Names: Wipfli, Jon, author.
Title: Venison : the Slay to Gourmet field to kitchen cookbook / Jon Wipfli: photography by Matt Lien.
Description: Minneapolis, MN : Voyageur Press, 2017. | Includes index.
Identifiers: LCCN 2017015689 | ISBN 9780760352403 (hardback)
Subjects: LCSH: Venison. | Slay to Gourmet (Catering service) | BISAC: SPORTS & RECREATION / Hunting. | COOKING / Specific Ingredients / Meat. | HOUSE & HOME / Sustainable Living. | LCGFT: Cookbooks.
Classification: LCC TX556.V4 W57 2017 | DDC 641.6/91--dc23
LC record available at https://lccn.loc.gov/2017015689

Acquiring Editor: Dennis Pernu
Project Manager: Alyssa Lochner
Art Director: Brad Springer
Cover Designer: Simon Larkin
Layout: Amy Sly

Printed in China

CONTENTS

Preface *8*

PART 1
THE HUNT
12

PART 2
BUTCHERY
20

PART 3
RECIPES
44

SHAREABLES

>>> — • — <<<

Heart Skewers WITH GARLIC, GINGER, AND CHILE OIL... 50

Leg Skewers WITH STOVETOP BEANS AND GREMOLATA... 54

Bone Broth 56

Cast-Iron-Seared Venison Dressed in Chile Honey
Mustard WITH FRY BREAD AND WINTER PICKLES 59

Meatballs WITH CHERRY BARBECUE SAUCE 62

Lettuce Wraps 64

Jalapeño Poppers WITH BROWN SUGAR–
BRAISED SHOULDER 66

Terrine WITH WINTER PICKLES, BACON JAM, AND CHILE
HONEY MUSTARD 68

Leg Sandwiches WITH BACON JAM AND CREAMY
BLUE CHEESE 71

Black and Blue Gut Loin Carpaccio WITH
GARLIC AIOLI 74

Roasted Shoulder, Seasoned Ricotta, and Chilled
Asparagus Salad WITH CHAMPAGNE VINAIGRETTE 76

Farro and Brussels Sprouts Soup WITH VENISON LEG ... 81

Venison Neck Split Pea Soup 84

Venison and Pineapple Chili 86

ENTRÉES

>>> — • — <<<

Breakfast Sausage WITH OVER-EASY EGGS
AND BACON BRUSSELS....................................... 91

Biscuits WITH COUNTRY-STYLE VENISON
SAUSAGE GRAVY... 95

Sausage Braise WITH SAUERKRAUT
AND BONE BROTH 99

Schnitzel WITH CREAMY KALE AND GRILLED LEMONS ... 100

Raw Kale Salad WITH LEG PAILLARD AND GARLIC,
ANCHOVY, AND HERB VINAIGRETTE 110

Smoked Leg Steak WITH COLESLAW 112

Burgers WITH SWEET POTATO FRIES
AND CHIMICHURRI.. 115

Tacos WITH JOSIE'S PICO DE GALLO, FENNEL CABBAGE
SLAW, AND GARLIC AIOLI................................. 121

Meatloaf WITH EMBER-ROASTED ROOT VEGETABLES
AND BOURBON-MAPLE BUTTER 126

Cori's Hot Dish 131

Blackened Sirloin WITH BLISTERED GREEN BEANS
AND HERB VINAIGRETTE 132

Pan-Seared Loin WITH WHOLE ROASTED CAULIFLOWER,
CAULIFLOWER PURÉE, AND TOASTED BREADCRUMBS..... 141

Porcini-Encrusted Loin WITH MASHED POTATOES,
MEAT SAUCE, AND WINTER PICKLES.................... 147

Lomo Al Trapo WITH SEARED BOK CHOY
AND ANCHOVY BUTTER 152

Roasted Tenderloin WITH WARM BACON AND SPINACH
SALAD 158

Butter-Poached Tenderloin WITH SAUCE GRIBICHE
AND SEARED ZUCCHINI 160

Tomato-and-Brown-Sugar-Braised Shoulder
WITH WHITE CHEDDAR AND JALAPEÑO GRITS............... 162

Shoulder Steak Confit WITH CARAMELIZED CABBAGE,
MEAT SAUCE, AND CHAMPAGNE VINAIGRETTE 165

Whole Confit Deer Leg WITH GRILLED FLATBREAD, FRUIT
COMPOTE, COMPOUND BUTTER, AND PESTO 168

Index *172*

About the Author and Acknowledgments *176*

PREFACE

By

NICK SCHIEFELBEIN

Venison is a cookbook for deer hunters, novice or veteran, and for anyone interested in one of our nation's oldest traditions. The whitetail deer happens to be the most sought-after big-game animal in the United States. They can be found in most of the lower forty-eight states and have a population of over thirty million. The whitetail is also among the most adaptable of big-game species, surviving in the forests of the Northeast and Midwest, the semiarid landscapes of the Southwest, and the prairies of the plains states.

That said, the recipes in this book can easily be adapted to other members of the deer family, from mule deer and pronghorn antelope to elk and even moose.

Currently, those men and women who identify themselves as deer hunters number somewhere in the neighborhood of ten million. In the past, the deer-hunting population came from a predominantly rural background, but as our country's demographics have shifted, so has the hunting community. Today, hunters come from all walks of life; as many call the city their home as do the country. They are a diverse group, not unlike their prey.

Hunters' motivations for pursuing game varies as much as they do. Much of the literature published and television shows produced for deer hunters are geared toward trophy hunting. Like it or not, there is no doubt that this is the direction the deer-hunting industry is headed. But to assume all deer hunters are driven by the prospect of a heavily racked buck that will put them in the record books is false. For many deer hunters, the primary motivation is simple: venison.

Now more than ever people are putting a greater value on where their food comes from. The slow-food revolution has sparked an interest in organic and sustainable food sources. Nothing is better suited to that model than hunting wild meat. Attitudes toward hunting are ever evolving, but the notion that harvesting your own meat is barbaric or somehow backward couldn't be further from the truth. To put it bluntly, if you really want to know where your food comes from and how it was processed, then kill it, butcher it, and enjoy the fruits (meats) of your labor.

With that in mind, prepare to enjoy an insightful step-by-step guide to turning your wild game into gourmet-quality table fare. The book is broken down into chapters that reflect the chronology in which a hunter procures his or her venison, butchers it, and finally prepares it. Therefore, we start at the beginning, the hunt, and a discussion of ethics and responsibility.

Chapter two covers the more technical aspects of butchering the animal after it has been harvested. It is important to note that, as with the old adage, "There's more than one way to skin a cat," there is also more than one way to skin a deer. The same goes for the butchering process. Presented here, however, is the method that was taught to the author and which has proved effective for him.

The last chapter gets down to the nitty-gritty. An in-depth look at recipes that use good ingredients and perhaps some cooking techniques that are new to you and which bring out all the flavor potential of your venison. Whether blacktails, mulies, or the ever-popular whitetails are currently filling your freezer, these recipes will not disappoint.

PART 1

THE HUNT

Before you get into this book, I want to be up front with some facts that might leave you wondering why you bought it or picked it up in the first place. First, I'm not a great hunter, chef, or writer, yet somehow you are holding a hunting and cooking book written by me in your hands. That said, I *have* put a great deal of thought and effort into getting better at all these things, and the results have made my life much more fulfilling.

That's what I want to pass on to you.

I was raised in a hunting family but did not begin taking the sport seriously until I was in my mid-twenties. Although many times I would end a day in the field empty-handed, the experiences kept me going back. The camaraderie among family and friends, the peacefulness of solitude, and the lessons learned out there all made coming home empty-handed worth the effort. Slowly, after years of practice, my failures taught me how to be successful and my freezer began to fill up with game. If nothing else, I hope this will encourage anyone interested in hunting to give it a try and to persevere through failure.

If you are looking for guidance or advice, it may be worthwhile to spend some time at a local gun club or at an event sponsored by a sporting group such as Pheasants Forever. You will find plenty of like-minded people interested in the art of hunting. And hunters, especially those who have enjoyed a cocktail or two, are usually eager to share their stories from the field. If you are one of the lucky ones, you may be let in on some safeguarded tips that only experienced hunters have learned throughout the years. I venture to say that you may even find yourself some new friends along the way.

ETHICS

The conversation of ethics and hunting cannot be ignored. Anti-hunting groups and hunters have been pushing their agendas for decades. Like any debate, there is validity to the arguments on both sides. Even though I generally do not agree with the anti-hunting agenda, its proponents offer some valuable talking points. History has proven that with a lack of hunting regulations, mankind is able to decimate a species to the point of extinction. Additionally, there is evidence of an extreme few hunters who have shown no signs of mercy, sportsmanlike behavior, or empathy in the act of killing. Undeniably, this reflects poorly on hunters as a whole. To counteract this, I recommend two critical considerations be taken into account before hunting game:

1. KILL EFFICIENTLY.
2. EAT WHAT YOU KILL.

There is much more that could be said of these recommendations; however, the purpose of offering these simple and obvious takeaways is to help anchor your hunting experiences, both morally and ethically. The hunting community will continue to be viewed more positively when we all attend to these guidelines with intention and heart.

EATING

After the kill comes the butchering, and after the butchering comes the reward—the meals you provide for yourself, your family, and your friends.

The recipe section in the book is intended to be approachable and used by any average at-home cook. I have included techniques and ingredients that may be new to you. Please do not be intimidated. The main goal is to use fresh, high-quality ingredients that match the quality of meat you successfully brought back from the field. Use the recipes verbatim if you'd like, but it's important to implement changes that you see fit. Add herbs, acidity, and salt to taste—there's no wrong answer in cooking. To that point, if you would like to substitute a different protein for venison, please do. Most of these recipes translate well to other meats. Always remember that whether you harvested the meat yourself or bought it from a butcher, a life was taken to provide your meal, so treat it well.

To summarize, get out into the woods. Practice, prepare, be ethical, and be flexible for any scenario that may arise. Have fun and don't be discouraged if you leave empty-handed. When you make a kill, treat it with respect and do your best to use the entire animal. The animal died to provide for you. Make good food.

PART 2

BUTCHERY

BUTCHER YOUR OWN

Butchery can be tough, but more than that, it can feel like an intimidating task to take on by yourself or even with another person. There is always the fear of cutting a muscle incorrectly, ruining the best cut, or generally doing a hack job.

At the end of the day, the benefits of taking the time to butcher your own deer outweigh all these fears. First, you undoubtedly know you are eating the deer you killed, unlike when you drop it off at a processor. Second, you can get super-specific cuts that meet your culinary needs. Finally, you also more intimately get to know the animal you killed. Scouting, stalking, and killing are the first steps to putting game on your table, but butchering your own animal brings the process to an entirely different level.

My goal here is to tell you that, once you successfully get past the gutting, you cannot mess up butchery. It's simply not possible. You may miss out on a specific cut or cut too far into a certain area, but that's absolutely okay as long as you know how to use that meat for another purpose. For example, let's say you want to make steaks out of the gut loin but you accidentally make a few cuts into the loin while taking it out, rendering it unusable for steaks. Rather than get frustrated, shift gears and prep the meat into medium-sized skewers, serve them with one of the many sauces in this book, and you're set. Honestly, many of the best dishes I've created have resulted from mistakes like this. It makes you think outside your usual structure and allows you to try something new. Oftentimes, mistakes turn out to be blessings.

OPPOSITE: Be sure to set up your hoist and gambrel on a branch sturdy and high enough to raise the deer's head off the ground.

GUTTING

Text and Photos by Phil Hasheider

There are roughly ten steps for dressing a big-game animal in the field.

1. Place the carcass on its back with the rump lower than the shoulders, and spread the legs.

2. If not mounting the head, cut from the sternum (breastbone) up the neck to the base of the jaw. Don't cut the windpipe yet; this cut will expose the windpipe and allow you to remove as much of it as possible later. The windpipe sours rapidly and is a leading cause of tainted meat.

3. Cut along the centerline of the belly from breastbone to the base of the tail. Cut the hide first and then return and make a cut through the belly muscle, along the same line, using your free hand to lift the skin and muscle away from the internal organs and intestines as you slice. Stop when you reach the aitchbone, which forms the joints in the pelvis.

4. Make a circular cut around the anus and free it from the hide. Draw it out of the pelvic cavity far enough to securely tie it shut with a heavy string. This will keep any feces from entering the body cavity when you release it.

5. Lay the carcass on its side. Loosen and roll out the stomach and intestines. Examine the liver. Keep it for sausage making if it looks healthy and free of spots, cysts, or scarring, which may indicate parasites or disease. If any are present, discard it. If clean, place the liver in a plastic bag and put it on ice as soon as possible.

6. The diaphragm separates the chest and stomach cavities. Cut around its edge and then split the breastbone. Any parts of the diaphragm that remain can be removed later.

7. Cut the esophagus near the jaw and pull the lungs, heart, and windpipe toward you and remove them from the body cavity. Cut any remaining tissues that hold it to the inside cavity.

8. Remove the heart and place it in a bag with the liver and cool as soon as possible.

9. Drain any excess blood from the body cavity by rolling the carcass over, or hanging it head-up to let it drain.

10. Use a clean cloth or paper towels to wipe down the inside of the body cavity. The carcass is now ready to be moved.

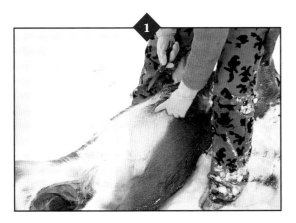

Field dress the animal immediately to drain the blood and dissipate the body heat. Wearing rubber gloves will make cleanup easier and protect you from any parasites or blood-borne diseases the animal may be carrying. Locate the base of the breastbone and make a shallow cut that is long enough to insert the first two fingers of your hand, being careful not to puncture the intestines.

Form a V with the first two fingers of your hand. Hold the knife between your fingers with the cutting edge up. Cut through the abdominal wall to the pelvic area, using your fingers to keep from puncturing the intestines.

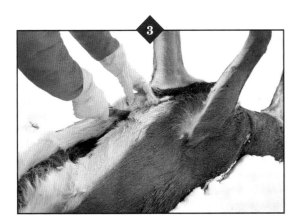

Straddle the animal, facing its head. If you do not plan to mount the head, cut the skin from the base of the breastbone to the jaw, with the cutting edge of the knife up. If you plan to mount the head, follow your taxidermist's instructions.

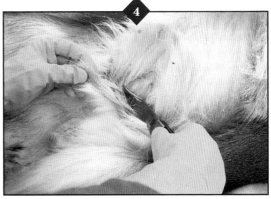

Separate the external reproductive organs of a buck from the abdominal wall, but do not cut them off completely. Remove the udder of a doe if it was still nursing— the milk sours rapidly and could give the meat an unpleasant flavor.

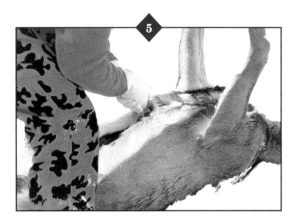

Cut through the center of the breastbone by bracing your elbows against your legs with one hand supporting the other; use your knees to provide leverage. An older animal may require a game saw or small axe.

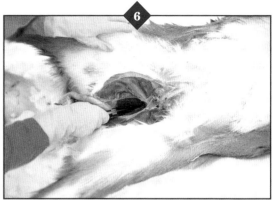

To free a deer's urethra, split the pelvic bone (or slice between the hams on a buck). Make careful cuts around the urethra until it is freed to a point just above the anus. Be careful not to sever the urethra. Cut around the anus; on a doe, the cut should also include the vulva above the anus. Free the rectum and urethra by loosening the connective tissue with your knife. Tie off the rectum and urethra with sturdy string to prevent fecal contamination of the inside body cavity.

Free the windpipe and esophagus by cutting the connective tissue. Sever the windpipe and esophagus at the jaw. Grasp them firmly and pull down, continuing to cut where necessary, until they are freed to the point where the windpipe branches out into the lungs.

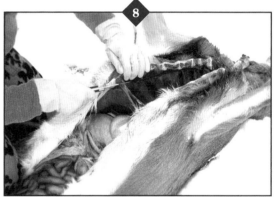

Hold the rib cage open on one side. Cut the diaphragm from the rib opening down to the backbone. Stay as close to the rib cage as possible; do not puncture the stomach. Repeat on the other side so that the cuts meet over the backbone.

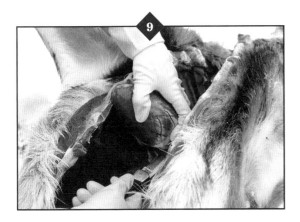

Remove the heart by severing the connecting blood vessels. Hold the heart upside down for a few moments to drain excess blood, then place it in a plastic bag. Some hunters find it easier to remove the viscera first before taking the heart and liver from it.

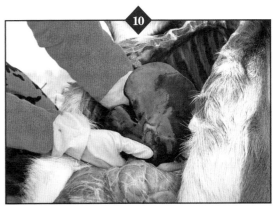

Cut the tubes that attach the liver and remove it. Check for spots, cysts, or scarring, which may indicate parasites or disease. If any are present, discard the liver. If the liver is clean, place into a plastic bag with the heart. Place on ice as soon as possible.

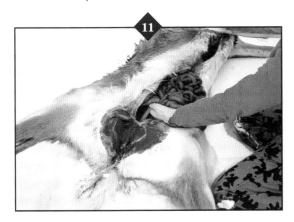

Pull the tied-off rectum and urethra from the pelvic bone and into the body cavity, unless you split the pelvic bone, making this unnecessary. Roll the carcass on its side so that the viscera begin to spill out the side of the body cavity.

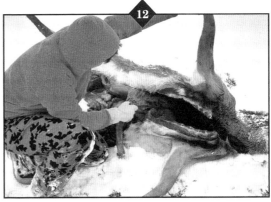

Firmly grasp the windpipe and esophagus; pull down and away from the body. If the organs do not pull away freely, the diaphragm may still be partially attached. Scoop from both ends toward the middle to finish rolling out the viscera.

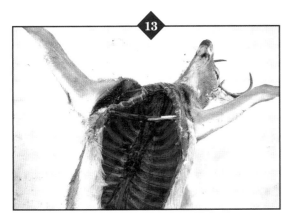

Sponge the cavity clean and prop open with a stick. If the urinary tract or intestines have been severed, wash the carcass with snow or clean water. If you need to leave the carcass, drape it over brush or logs with the cavity down, or hang it from a tree to speed cooling.

SKINNING

The old saying that there are a thousand ways to skin a cat goes for deer too. Everyone seems to have a method that gets the job done equally as well as the next guy's version. My way requires a sharp knife, a deer hoist, a gambrel, and a bone saw. This is how it goes in six easy steps:

1. Set up your hoist and gambrel on a solid branch (or a garage rafter) that is high enough to bring the deer head completely off the ground. Make incisions behind both Achilles tendons and insert the gambrel into the incisions. Hoist the deer off the ground.

2. Once the deer is up, make incisions around the circumference of the rear leg through the skin just below the Achilles. On the inside of the leg, connect the circumference cut to the cuts made from gutting the deer. Note: Your cuts should only be hide deep; do not cut into the meat or through the Achilles.

3. At the points where the circumference cuts on each leg meet the starting points of the cuts leading to the gut opening, take your knife and cut the hide away from the flesh. A little corner is all you need to start the process.

4. Now that there's small corner of hide pulling away from the meat, use your fingers to pull that away from the leg and use long strokes with your knife to make the flap increasingly larger. Work slowly, making your way around each circumference cut and down around the legs. Work evenly, taking hide away equally down from the tail to the snout.

5. Continue this process, letting flaps of hide curl down backward off the deer until you're all the way to the front legs. There will be points on the deer where it's easier to pull the skin away rather than use your knife; this technique will save you a significant amount of time. When you get to the front legs, use the same process as you used on the rear legs to remove hide from the legs.

6. Cut the hide as far down the neck toward the head as possible and saw off the head. Set the head and hide aside for the tanner and taxidermist.

SKINNING TIPS

1. Pull the hide while you're cutting. You'll be able to see where you need to cut better, and it will also speed up the process.

2. When running your knife, angle the blade away from the flesh and slightly into hide. This will help prevent cuts into the meat.

3. If possible, let the carcass cool to as close to 35°F (2°C) as possible. Do not let it freeze. The meat will be firmer and easier to work with.

Hang the deer on your gambrel from a sturdy limb or rafter to a height that is comfortable for you to work on the carcass, head to tail.

Initial incisions are made through the hide around the circumference of each rear leg just below (as the deer hangs) the Achilles tendons.

On the inside of each leg, connect the circumference cuts to the opening made from gutting the deer.

Take care that your cuts are only hide-deep and do not cut the meat. A little corner is all you need to begin the process of removing the hide. Sometimes it will be easier to simply pull the hide away from the deer.

Work slowly to cut between hide and flesh, letting flaps of hide curl down backward off the deer until you're all the way to the front legs.

The hide completely removed up to the neck. Cut the front leg similarly to the rear—run your knife down the leg until it hits the point to which the hide has been pulled down.

BREAKDOWN

Butchering any large animal is much more manageable if you break the animal down into smaller parts rather than try to tackle the entire animal in one go. I break down my deer into six sections and then separate muscles off of these. This breakdown is into hindquarters, middles, and forequarters, all three of which get split down the spine, yielding six sections. Before getting to any of that, though, it's best to remove the gut loins and backstraps to maximize their yields.

The gut loins are located inside the cavity, one on each side of the spinal column toward the rear of the animal. Oftentimes they can be removed by hand. Carefully wedge your fingers behind each gut loin and gently pull it off the carcass, one at a time.

There's also one backstrap, more commonly referred to in the kitchen as a loin, on each side of the carcass running down the entire midsection of the animal along the exterior of spine. Using a sharp knife, make incisions from the top of the backstrap to the bottom along the spine. Pull the backstrap away from the spine and cut it away from the ribs using long strokes of your knife. This will have a somewhat natural ending spot where the cut effortlessly detaches from the rest of the carcass.

Make incisions from the top of the backstrap to the bottom along the spine. Pull the backstrap away from the spine and cut it away from the ribs using long strokes.

One backstrap removed—certainly a prize cut from any deer!

An excellent view of the incisions made to remove the backstraps.

Initial incisions into the ribs are the first step in removing the forequarters. Counting from the head end, find the space between the fifth and sixth ribs. From inside the carcass, run your knife up to the spine and down to the bottom of the ribcage on both sides of the animal. This will leave the forequarters hanging by the spine. Use a bone saw to cut through the spine.

Removing the middles takes a small amount of guesswork. I start a little bit down (up on the hanging carcass) from where the backstraps ended, just north of where the spine starts to curve. Use a boning knife here to cut through protein attaching the two sections. Cut through the spine with a bone saw.

The muscles are now broken into manageable sections.

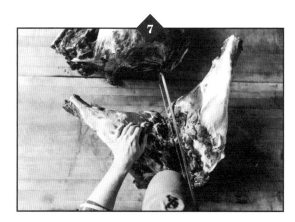

Using a saw, cut right down the middle of the hindquarter so that you're left with two equal halves. This can be done with the hindquarters still hanging on the gambrel or it can be done back in the garage or kitchen.

The muscles further broken into six easily workable sections: two fores (with the legs removed, bottom right), two middles (center), and two hinds (left). The shoulders are at upper right.

FOREQUARTERS

Counting from the head end on the inside of the carcass, find the space between the fifth and the sixth rib. Insert your knife from the inside of the carcass between these ribs and run it up to the spine and then back down to the bottom of the ribcage. Do this on both sides of the animal.

Once this is complete, the forequarters should be hanging by only the spine. Use a bone saw to cut through the spine, separating the forequarters from the rest of the carcass. On a cutting board, lay the forequarters spine down with the ribcage opening up and saw down the middle of the spine, creating two equal halves. Clean up any bone shavings on the meat and set the sections in a cold area until ready to break down further.

MIDDLES

Taking off the middles in this style takes a small amount of guesswork on where exactly to cut. From years of experience of breaking down animals, I have a pretty good idea of where the spine starts to curve down, which is where I like to separate the middle from the hindquarters. Another way to locate this spot, or get pretty damn close to it, is by cutting just a little bit down from where the backstrap ended. I'd look for an area to make a cut that's not going to cut into the hindquarters but still takes off any remaining ribcage and belly. Pick out your spot and use a boning knife to cut through any protein that would attach the two sections. Once that's cut, use a bone saw to cut through the spine. Again, lay the section spine-side down and cut down the middle of the spine to create two even halves. Set in a cool area until ready to break down further.

The forequarters, or shoulders, require the most finesse to prepare properly. Cut around the shank, leg, and scapula or paddle. Try to keep the chunks as large as possible to be broken down later or kept large.

The paddle (upper right) in the process of being removed from one of the fores.

Meat is scraped from the paddle. The richly marbled nature of the fore makes it ideal for grinding.

The silver skin is cleaned from the loins, using a sharp filet or boning knife.

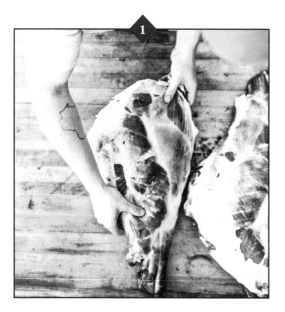

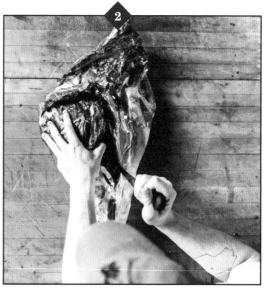

The hindquarters offer a lot of opportunities for great roasts and flavorful steaks. You'll find much less connective tissue and fat to deal with than you will in the fores.

On the inside of each leg, run your knife directly over the length of the leg bone up to the ball joint. With the tip of your knife, slowly carve around the leg bone and tailbone until the leg bone is free from the muscle.

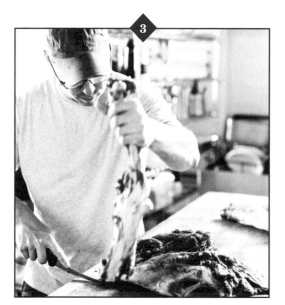

Removing the bones from a hindquarter.

With the bones removed from the leg, place the open side up like a book. Feel around for seams in the muscles that seem to naturally separate. They'll all be separated by silver skin. Once you locate one, use tip of your knife to break off larger muscle groups.

Examples of some larger muscles cut from the legs.

HINDQUARTERS

You'll now be left with hanging hindquarters, which need to be split and then sawed from where you made your initial cut to start removing hide. Use your knife to cut any meat that would get in the way of making a clean cut down the middle of the hindquarter. Using a saw, cut right down the middle of the hindquarter so that you're left with two equal halves. Then cut each of them just under where they're hanging from and pull them off of the gambrel. Your deer is now in six manageable sections.

THE SECTIONS

As a rule, before you start to break down individual muscle groups, make sure that the meat is free and clear of any fur or other debris. It's much easier to remove debris before the muscles are reduced to small cuts. Also, if desired, do any trimming of fat while the muscles are in big sections. I keep as much fat on the muscles as possible, but that's a personal preference. Finally, use a sharp and semiflexible boning knife and a small bone saw to make the process go much more smoothly.

FOREQUARTERS

The forequarters, or shoulders, hold some of the best-tasting muscles in the animal. That section is loaded with fat that marbles the protein. It also contains a significant amount of connective tissue, which equals more flavor. That being said, these muscles can take the most finesse to prepare properly, but once they're mastered, they will produce the best meals. I cannot overemphasize how important it is to not just put the entire shoulder into the meat grinder for burger or sausage—you will end up with a large enough amount of scrap for just that anyway.

Before you begin cutting, lay the entire leg on your cutting board and study how it would function on a living and breathing deer and where the bones lie within the cut. There will be a neck bone that connects itself to the ribcage. On the outside of the ribcage, you have the shank, leg bone, and the scapula (paddle). Once you have a mental image of where the bones rest in the muscles, figure out what cuts you'd like to get out of the shoulder. I like to get a few larger roasts, some larger chunks to dice into braising meat, and some smaller pieces that I can finely mince for lettuce wraps or tacos.

Start by cutting off the neck, using your boning knife to cut through all the protein and the saw to cut through the bone. Set the neck aside for a braise, a roast, or smoking. Remove the ribcage by running your knife down and under the ribs and back out the opposite side. Make small incisions with your knife facing toward the bone and continually work your knife closely to the bone to keep as much protein intact as possible. Once the entire ribcage is loose, cut around the exterior of any neck muscles remaining and pull the ribcage out. Set it aside for stock and pick away scrap meat for grinding. The next bones to attack are the shank, leg, and paddle. Cut off the entire shank and set it aside for a braise or for scrap. Next, cut off the large muscle on the top of the shoulder, which would be considered the Boston butt. This is a great, larger-sized cut to put away for a roast or a long smoke. Finally, cut around all the remaining bones, removing chunks as large as possible. These can be broken down later or kept large depending on what you want them for. Reserve the bones for scrap and move on to the other leg.

OPPOSITE: *Scraps are ground for hamburger.*

Everything is laid out.

MIDDLES

Depending on what you'd like to get out of the middles, there are a few different ways to approach this section. Since you've already taken the backstraps out of the midsection, there aren't any large cuts of meat left on the middles. Oftentimes a kill shot will have penetrated the ribs, which can influence how to butcher them best. If the ribcage is free of entry and exit wounds, I recommend cutting individual ribs and smoking them. This requires keeping as much meat as possible on the ribcage during the initial butchering process, so if you want good ribs, keep that in mind when you're breaking down the carcass. If there are messy wounds in the ribcage, or if you don't have the equipment to make ribs, you can trim the meat away from the ribs and the diaphragm and use it as grinding meat. The last option is to use the entire rib section to make bone broths and stocks. Personally, I like to include a good amount of on-bone protein in my stocks to make them that much richer and full flavored.

HINDQUARTERS

The deer's hindquarters are also filled with a lot of opportunities to make great roasts and flavorful steaks. Unlike the forequarter, there is not nearly as much connective tissue or fat to deal with. Most of the cuts are relatively lean and can be used as steaks that do not require long cooking times. The bone structure in the hindquarter is also much simpler, with just a larger leg bone and a pelvis, both of which are easily removed.

Also, if you're feeding a large group, the entire leg bone can be left in and the leg can be brined and turned into a ham or salt cured and cooked slowly in a large pan covered by butter. This is a very quick way to make a lot of friends.

Again, before you begin cutting, take a look at the muscle as a whole and imagine where the bones lie in the animal and how the muscles and bones would operate on a living deer. The shank connects to the leg bone, which runs up the center of the muscle, where it connects via a ball joint to the pelvis. Cut off the shanks and set them aside with the front shanks. Next, on the inside of the leg, run your knife directly over the length of the leg bone up to the ball joint. With the tip of your knife, slowly carve around the bone until the leg bone is free from the muscle. Release the leg bone from the ball joint and set it aside. Next, carefully cut out the remainder of the pelvis by working your knife as closely to the bone as possible. With your fingers, feel where the bone goes before making cuts and simply follow the curves of the bone. Once the pelvis is removed, set it aside with the rest of the bones for stock.

Now that the bones are out of the leg, place the open side up so it's facing you like an open book. Feel around the muscles and find seams that seem to naturally separate. There are a few of these seams throughout the leg, and all are separated by silver skin. Once one is located, use the tip of your knife to break off larger muscle groups. You should end up with five or six different large groups depending on how far they were broken down. Most of these muscles will be lean, but the groups closer to the foot will have more connective tissue and silver skin than the rest. I like to grind these for burger or sausage. Trim the rest of the muscles of excess silver skin and break them into cuts that you'd like to have on hand. These steaks are pretty lean and great for schnitzel, pan searing, stir-fries, or anything with a hot and fast cook time.

PART 3

RECIPES

If there's one thing I wish I would have learned earlier as a chef, it's that most recipes (those for baked goods not included) are meant to be used as guidelines, not gospel. Throughout this book and many other cookbooks, you will see sayings such as "a pinch of salt" or "a half lemon," measurements that will vary depending on the cook or the product being used. Across the board, ingredients have different characteristics and may only reach their full potential when the person preparing them makes adjustments while cooking.

For example, a recipe that calls for beets might be affected by how sweet the beets are when you get them; the pork you're grinding into your venison sausage might be leaner than the pork at a grocery store a mile away, creating a less fatty blend; or the vinegar in your pantry might be more or less acidic than the one I used while creating these recipes. Furthermore, individual palates vary greatly, making it nearly impossible to write a recipe that perfectly suits everyone's needs.

To balance these natural variables in food and in people, I encourage you to taste, taste, and taste again while preparing your food to make it suit your individual needs. Think about the flavors as you're tasting and cooking. Rather than thinking about food as ingredients, break their characteristics into flavor groups that need to be balanced. There are six main flavor areas to think of when tasting: salt, sweet, sour, bitter, spice, and umami (savory). If the dish is too rich, add some acidity (e.g., lemon juice) to balance it. If it's too salty add some fat (e.g., heavy cream), or if it's tasting flat add some salt to make it pop. Not only will you start to enjoy the dishes you create more, but you'll start to have a deeper understanding about how a truly great-tasting dish is created, and you'll have the tools to start developing mouthwatering recipes on your own.

I hope that this book will guide you to new yet simple techniques and different types of produce that you haven't used with game. With that knowledge in hand, I hope the final tweaks to these dishes will be put together through experimentation by you. I'll get you 90 percent of the way to a great recipe, but the last 10 percent will be decided by your willingness to experiment, fail, and learn. At the end of the day, don't take it too seriously—it's just food. Drink a beer while you cook, use good ingredients, and cook as much food as possible for your friends and family, and every time you step into your kitchen will be a good time.

SHAREABLES

There's nothing quite like a table full of appetizers to really make for a good dinner party, and these recipes are intended for exactly that. The interactive nature of these recipes keeps the atmosphere light while giving your guests something to talk about. On top of that, you'll be able to showcase your culinary prowess.

Heart Skewers
with Garlic, Ginger, and Chile Oil

This is a pretty simple recipe, but when done correctly, it is fantastic. It all comes down to cooking the protein correctly. Make sure that your grill grates are clean, hot, and wiped down with a thin layer of oil to help prevent sticking. These simple tips will help your grill game dramatically!

HEART SKEWERS

INGREDIENTS

1 venison heart

PROCEDURE

Begin by getting your grill nice and hot. Clean the heart of any fat and white veins. Dice it into roughly ½-inch cubes and place the cubes on skewers, 4 to 5 pieces per for each presoaked bamboo skewer. Place the skewers on your grill and try to flip them only once while cooking them to medium rare.

GARLIC, GINGER, AND CHILE OIL

INGREDIENTS

½ cup grapeseed oil

5 Thai chiles, thinly sliced

2-inch knob fresh ginger, peeled and diced

2 garlic cloves, minced

PROCEDURE

In a sauté pan, combine the oil, chiles, ginger, and garlic, and place the pan on the stove over medium-low heat. Slowly cook the aromatics until they just begin to brown, about 6 minutes. Then immediately pull the pan off the heat. The oil can be stored in the refrigerator in a tightly sealed jar for up to 1 week.

TO FINISH

Pull the skewers off the grill to a plate and give them a solid brushing of the garlic, ginger, and chile oil and serve immediately.

This recipe will also work with cuts from the leg. If using leg, cut the steak into bite-size chunks (about ¾ inch by ¾ inch) that are easily pierced by the skewer without breaking and follow the same procedure as above.

LEG SKEWERS
WITH STOVETOP BEANS AND GREMOLATA

I love skewers and I love beans—and together the two create a nice plated appetizer. Find some small cubes or slices of leg and pack them tightly onto soaked bamboo skewers. My alternative to taking the time to soak and cook dried beans is to doctor up canned beans. Either method can be delicious, but this stovetop version is quick and packs a lot of flavor, while the gremolata adds a layer of freshness. You can prep the beans and gremolata ahead of time and reheat them while grilling the skewers for a great camp snack!

LEG SKEWERS

INGREDIENTS

32 small cubed pieces (about ¾ inch by ¾ inch) venison leg

Kosher salt and freshly cracked pepper to taste

PROCEDURE

Tightly pack the venison onto the skewers, using 4 cubes of meat per skewer for a total of 8 skewers. Lightly salt them. On a hot grill, cook the skewers roughly 4–5 minutes until they have an internal temperature of 130°F (54°C), rotating them so that they have even, dark grill marks on all sides.

STOVETOP BEANS

INGREDIENTS

2 strips smoked bacon, cut into lardons

1 small yellow onion, diced

1 clove garlic, thinly sliced

1 jalapeño, small diced

¼ cup brown sugar

1 teaspoon ground cumin

½ cup Bone Broth (page 56) or chicken stock

2 (15-ounce) cans butter beans, drained

1 tablespoon butter

1 tablespoon chopped parsley

Kosher salt

PROCEDURE

Place a medium sauté pan over medium heat and add the bacon lardons to the pan. Stir the bacon lardons until they are starting to brown and the fat is rendered. Add the onion, garlic, and jalapeño and cook until the onion is translucent, about 6 minutes. Add the brown sugar and cumin and cook until the sugar is melted. Add the bone broth and the beans and warm until the sauce becomes incorporated, about 5 more minutes. Add the butter and parsley; let the butter melt into the sauce, stir, then salt to taste.

BONE BROTH

Stocks and broths are the foundations of all great cooking. This is a very simple recipe that can also be used with other animal bones and will transform your cooking from good to great. Throughout the book, I have included recipes that call for this particular venison broth or chicken stock, but you can feel free to substitute any stock that you have on hand. Homemade is always better than store-bought, but either will do. One easy use of this broth is to reduce it further by half after the fat is skimmed off, season it with a little bit of red pepper flakes and salt, and drink it like coffee.

INGREDIENTS

3 pounds venison bones

Cold water

PROCEDURE

Preheat the oven to 350°F (176°C). Arrange the bones on a large rimmed baking sheet and roast until they are very dark brown but not black. Check the bones after 30 minutes and then every 15 minutes until the desired color is reached.

Place the bones in a large stockpot and cover them with cold water. Bring the mixture to a soft simmer over medium heat, then reduce the heat to low and keep at a soft simmer for 24 hours. Skim off and discard any foam that forms at the top. Add water throughout the simmering process whenever the water level dips below the bones, and try to reduce the total amount of liquid by one-third for a strong, hearty broth.

Strain through a fine mesh strainer into a sealable container and place the liquid in the refrigerator overnight. After the liquid has cooled, the fat will have solidified at the top. Skim it off and discard. Portion the remaining broth into containers and freeze until needed.

GREMOLATA

INGREDIENTS

1 clove garlic

¼ cup parsley

Zest of one orange

PROCEDURE

Finely mince the garlic and parsley and place in a small bowl. Add the zest, and combine.

TO FINISH

Place a few ladlefuls of the beans into each shallow bowl. Place two skewers on top of the beans in each bowl and sprinkle some gremolata over the dish. Eat with a spoon, getting some beans and some venison in each bite.

Cast-Iron–Seared Venison
Dressed in Chile Honey Mustard with Fry Bread and Winter Pickles

A few different cuts are interchangeable for this dish. Any lean steak from the loin (backstrap), gut loin, or hindquarters will do.

While homemade bread is great, it's fairly time consuming and takes a skilled hand to master. Fry bread is an easy and fun alternative to traditional bread, and it makes for fantastic individual appetizers.

These pickles can be made quickly. Most of the time spent on them should be used to make the vegetables uniform shapes and sizes. This will add a refined look to the plate and also ensure the ingredients are evenly pickled. The pickles are great to have on hand to garnish any protein, so make extra if you can—they'll stay good for months in your refrigerator.

One final note: when preparing this dish, it's best to start with the bread and pickles.

SEARED VENISON

INGREDIENTS

1 pound venison steak (from the loin, gut loin, or hindquarters)

Grapeseed oil

Kosher salt and pepper

PROCEDURE

Heat a cast-iron pan over medium-high heat, and add enough grapeseed oil to cover the bottom of the pan. While that's heating, season the steak with salt and pepper. When the pan is hot, place the steak in the pan and sear it on all sides until it has an internal temperature of at least 130°F (54°C). Remove the steak from the pan and let it rest for about 5 minutes.

FRY BREAD

INGREDIENTS

2 cups all-purpose flour

1 tablespoon baking powder

1 tablespoon kosher salt

1 tablespoon finely chopped
fresh thyme

1 tablespoon finely chopped
fresh sage

1 cup warm water

Grapeseed oil for frying and for
your hands

PROCEDURE

Mix the ingredients until they are completely incorporated and let
the dough sit for 30 minutes. Heat a ½ inch of grapeseed oil in a
sauté pan until just before it begins to smoke. While that's heating,
cover your hands in grapeseed oil to help the sticky dough release
from your hands and form the dough into patties roughly 2 inches
across and a ½ inch thick. Working in batches, place the patties in
the hot oil and fry until brown on one side, then flip and fry until
brown on the other side (approximately 1 minute on each side). Cut
one open to make sure the dough is cooked through. Keep warm
until the steak is done. The recipe should yield 10–12 patties.

CHILE HONEY MUSTARD DRESSING

INGREDIENTS

5 Thai chiles, finely minced

¼ cup honey, plus additional as
desired

2 tablespoons Dijon mustard, plus
additional as desired

PROCEDURE

Combine the chiles, honey, and mustard in a small bowl. Add
additional honey or mustard until you reach your desired flavor. The
dressing will keep in a refrigerator for a few weeks and can be used
in salads or as a sauce with other meats.

WINTER PICKLES

INGREDIENTS

- 2 cups apple cider vinegar
- 2 cups water
- 2 whole cloves
- 1 whole star anise
- 2 whole juniper berries
- Pinch of kosher salt
- Pinch of sugar
- 1 cup diced carrots
- 1 cup diced daikon radish
- 1 cup cauliflower florets
- 1 cup diced fennel

PROCEDURE

Bring the vinegar, water, cloves, star anise, juniper berries, salt, and sugar to a boil in a high-walled saucepan. Add the carrots, daikon radish, cauliflower, and fennel. When it returns to a boil, pull it off the heat and let the vegetables cool in the pickling liquid for at least 25 minutes before serving, or store them in the fridge in the pickling liquid inside a sealed plastic or glass container.

TO FINISH

Thinly slice the steak against the grain and place it into a mixing bowl. Pour dressing over the venison and toss the slices until they're generously coated. Use enough dressing so that some is leftover on the bottom of the mixing bowl—don't be shy with this! Pull or slice the fry bread buns apart at the middle and fill with a few slices of marinated venison and a small spoonful of pickles.

Winter Pickles

MEATBALLS
WITH CHERRY BARBECUE SAUCE

The flavor and texture of venison often benefits from the addition of ground pork shoulder, and this recipe is a perfect example. Using a 50/50 blend of venison and ground pork will leave you with a more succulent, less gamey meatball.

MEATBALLS

INGREDIENTS

Grapeseed oil to evenly coat the bottom of your pan, plus additional for greasing the pan

1 white onion, small diced

1 clove garlic, small diced

1 tablespoon minced fresh thyme

½ teaspoon ground cloves

½ teaspoon ground juniper berries

2 cups fresh white breadcrumbs (from about 12 slices of bread)

1 cup whole milk (do not substitute low-fat milk)

1 pound ground venison shoulder

1 pound ground pork

2 eggs

½ tablespoon kosher salt

PROCEDURE

Place the oil, onion, garlic, thyme, cloves, and juniper berries in a sauté pan and slowly cook over very low heat until all the moisture from the vegetables is gone and they are completely soft, making sure that there are no colors developed in the pan while cooking, about 45 minutes Once cooked, transfer the vegetables to a mixing bowl and let them cool in the fridge. Next, take the 12 slices of bread, remove their crusts, and mince them into tiny crumbs. In a separate mixing bowl, add the breadcrumbs and pour the milk over the bread slowly until it looks like a mucky swamp bottom. The bread should absorb all the liquid, and there shouldn't be any excess. If there is excess milk, pour it out of the bowl and discard it. Place that mixing bowl in the refrigerator to keep it cool. Place the venison and pork into the bowl of a stand mixer fitted with the paddle attachment. Add the bread-and-milk mixture along with the cooked vegetables and salt, and turn on the mixer to a medium-low speed. Add the eggs one at a time and mix until they're fully incorporated. Let the paddle spin for about a minute, or until you notice that the meat is starting to stick together on its own accord and is beginning to look gummy. At this point, remove a small patty of the meatball mix and pan-fry it. Taste it for salt and texture—it shouldn't be crumbling apart—and adjust the salt in the meatball mix if necessary. If your tester crumbled, continue mixing the meatball mixture until it becomes more cohesive.

Once the meatball mix is ready, preheat the oven to 450°F (232°C) and lightly coat a rimmed baking sheet with grapeseed oil. Roll the meatballs into 1½-ounce balls, just bigger than a half-dollar coin, place them on the sheet. Bake until they have an internal temperature of 155°F (68°C), about 20 minutes

CHERRY BARBECUE SAUCE

INGREDIENTS

2 tablespoons butter

1 yellow onion, small diced

2 cloves garlic, minced

1 tablespoon minced fresh ginger

¼ cup ketchup

1½ cups tomato sauce

1½ cups fresh pitted cherries

⅔ cup packed dark brown sugar

⅓ cup freshly squeezed orange juice

¼ cup champagne vinegar

1 tablespoon dried basil

1 teaspoon cayenne pepper

PROCEDURE

In a large pot over medium-low heat, melt the butter. Add the onions and cook until they appear slightly translucent, about 5 minutes. Add the garlic and cook for about 30 seconds. Add the remaining ingredients and stir to combine. Softly simmer until thickened, stirring occasionally, about 30 minutes. Place the sauce into a blender and blend until smooth. Add more orange juice if necessary to thin it out if the barbecue sauce is too thick.

TO FINISH

Poke a skewer into each meatball and dip the meatball halfway into a bowl of the cherry barbecue sauce and serve immediately on a plate, skewer side up for easy access.

LETTUCE WRAPS

This is a dish I could eat every day. It has bright Asian flavors, is just spicy enough to make me sweat, and is light enough for any meal or to share as an appetizer.

INGREDIENTS

½ cup hazelnuts

Grapeseed oil

1 pound ground venison shoulder

1-inch knob fresh ginger, minced

3 Thai chiles, minced

1 poblano pepper, minced

½ yellow onion, minced

1 clove garlic, minced

1 tablespoon chopped lemongrass

2 tablespoons packed brown sugar

1 tablespoon plus 2 teaspoons fish sauce

2 heads Boston, Bibb, or butter lettuce

1 cup cilantro leaves, chopped

Fresh lime slices, for serving

PROCEDURE

Preheat the oven to 350°F (177°C). Add the hazelnuts to a small rimmed baking sheet and toast them in the oven until the meat of the nut has begun to brown and they've become fragrant, about 15 minutes. When the nuts are just cool enough to handle, place them on one half of a flat kitchen towel, fold over the other side, and rub the hazelnuts until the skins have been removed from the nut. When the nuts are completely cool, roughly chop them into small pieces.

Heat a sauté pan over high heat. Add just enough grapeseed oil to cover the bottom of the pan. When the pan is hot, sear the venison until it's brown on one side, then stir to continue cooking. When the meat is cooked, remove it from the pan and set it aside. Add a bit more grapeseed oil to the pan, just to coat the bottom, and add the ginger, Thai chiles, poblano, onion, garlic, and lemongrass. Sauté for 45 seconds, just until the vegetables begin to soften. Add the brown sugar and fish sauce, and let that simmer for 3 to 4 minutes before adding the venison back to the pan. Heat until the venison is hot.

TO FINISH

Remove individual lettuce leaves from the head of lettuce and fill them with a scoop or two of the sautéed venison. Transfer to a plate and garnish with hazelnuts, cilantro, and a squeeze of fresh lime juice.

Jalapeño Poppers
WITH BROWN SUGAR-BRAISED SHOULDER

There are a few guilty-pleasure foods that I could snack on until my pants don't fit anymore, and jalapeño poppers are one of them. Who can turn away warm, seasoned cream cheese in a fresh jalapeño topped with braised meats and bacon? It's nearly impossible to say no. This recipe cross-references the Rib Rub recipe (see page 72) and the Tomato-and-Brown-Sugar-Braised Shoulder (page 162), making it a good way to use up any leftover meat from that dish.

INGREDIENTS

10 jalapeños, split in half the long way with seeds removed

½ pound softened cream cheese

¼ cup sour cream

1 teaspoon Rib Rub (see page 72)

½ pound leftover brown sugar–braised shoulder

20 thin slices of bacon

20 toothpicks

PROCEDURE

In a food processor, blend the cream cheese, sour cream, and rib rub until they're fully incorporated. With a spoon, evenly distribute the resulting mixture into the jalapeño halves so each is about ¾ full. Next, smash the braised venison shoulder a bit so the meat is crumbling. Finish filling the jalapeño halves with the smashed venison shoulder on top of the cream cheese mixture. Once the jalapeños are filled, wrap each half with a bacon strip and stick a toothpick through the jalapeño to hold the bacon in place. Bake the jalapeños at 375°F (191°C) for 15–20 minutes or until the bacon is crispy. Remove from the oven, place on a plate, and serve immediately.

TERRINE
WITH WINTER PICKLES, BACON JAM, AND CHILE HONEY MUSTARD

Terrines can be a pain in the butt to get just right. They can be finicky in so many ways, but when you nail them, the end results are special and rewarding. Always make a terrine in a water bath to create a gentler, more even cooking ambience. After cooking, press it evenly with a weight to help reduce crumbling while slicing. If it does crumble, just play it cool and spread it on bread—the flavors will still be incredible.

I serve it here with a few accoutrements that can be found elsewhere in the book (including the Chile Honey Mustard on page 60 and Winter Pickles page 61), but an endless number of garnishes will taste good with this terrine. Stoneground mustards, jams, or vegetable pickles always pair up well with a terrine. If desired, serve on toasted baguette slices or crunchy crackers.

TERRINE

INGREDIENTS

1 pound venison shoulder, diced

1 pound uncured pork belly, diced

8 ounces cleaned venison liver (chicken liver works too)

¼ cup chopped yellow onion

¼ cup minced parsley

1½ tablespoons minced garlic

1½ tablespoons kosher salt

1 teaspoon ground black pepper

½ tablespoon Chinese five-spice powder

2 large eggs

2 tablespoons brandy

PROCEDURE

Before you start, freeze all the grinding equipment for 45 minutes and preheat the oven to 275°F (135°C). Mix the pork belly, liver, onion, parsley, garlic, salt, black pepper, five-spice, eggs, and brandy, then run through a meat grinder with the ⅛-inch die attached. Replace the ⅛-inch die with a ⅜-inch die and run the venison through. Mix all the ingredients thoroughly.

Line a terrine or bread pan with plastic wrap, making sure to leave plastic wrap overhanging the sides by about 3 inches. Pour the meat mixture in and fold the excess plastic wrap over the top of the terrine. Place the pan in a larger baking pan that comes at least three-quarters of the way up the sides of the terrine pan. Add enough hot water to come about halfway up the terrine pan's walls. Carefully transfer the container to the oven and cook until the internal temperature of the terrine hits 155°F (68°C), about 1 hour.

Remove the terrine from the oven and place a 2- to 3-pound weight on the terrine. Let cool to room temperature. Keep the weight on and let it sit overnight in the refrigerator before serving.

BACON JAM

INGREDIENTS

1 pound bacon, chopped

4 yellow onions

2 tablespoons butter

½ cup packed brown sugar

½ cup apple cider vinegar

1 teaspoon kosher salt

2 teaspoons ground black pepper

PROCEDURE

Heat a heavy pot over medium heat and add the bacon and onions. When the fat has rendered from the bacon, add the butter, brown sugar, vinegar, salt, and pepper. Continue to cook, stirring occasionally, until the mixture becomes dark, about an hour. If the jam seems to be separating, add ¼ cup water to bring it back together. Remove from the heat and allow to cool slightly. Add additional salt and pepper to taste.

TO FINISH

Serve slices of the terrine alongside individual containers of the accoutrements, along with toasted baguette slices or crackers. Let your guests decide what to garnish each bite with.

LEG SANDWICHES
WITH BACON JAM AND CREAMY BLUE CHEESE

›››——————→ · ←——————‹‹‹

A beautiful sandwich is proof that there's a higher power, and this recipe is no exception. The result tastes good hot but can also be taken cold into the field for a high-class midday snack. There's not a lot of finesse here, just ingredients that taste really good piled onto other ingredients that taste really good. Bacon jam gives the sandwich a big hit of sweet and savory, while the blue cheese is creamy, fatty, and unctuous. Both the jam and cheese pair nicely with roasted slices of venison leg. Venison leg steaks work great here, either one large cut or a few smaller muscles.

Please refer to the Bacon Jam recipe accompanying the terrine on page 69.

LEG SANDWICHES

INGREDIENTS

Canola oil (or other high-temperature oil), for the grill

2 pounds venison leg steak

Rib Rub, enough to cover leg (about 3 tablespoons; see page 72)

Ground black pepper

Bacon Jam (see page 69)

Baguettes from your favorite bakery

PROCEDURE

First, heat your grill to a high temperature and give the grates a coat of oil. Evenly coat the steak with your rib rub and place it on the hottest spot on the grill. When there's a good sear on the bottom side, flip the steak and grill the other side until it has an internal temperature of 130°F (55°C). Pull the steak and let it rest before slicing.

RIB RUB

INGREDIENTS

½ cup smoked paprika

¼ cup kosher salt

¼ cup ground black pepper

¼ cup brown sugar

3 tablespoons ground cumin

3 tablespoons ground coriander

1 tablespoon red pepper flakes, ground

1 tablespoon garlic powder

PROCEDURE

Combine all ingredients in a mixing bowl. I recommend making a full batch of this and keeping it in your spice cabinet to use as needed; stored properly it will be good for a year.

CREAMY BLUE CHEESE

INGREDIENTS

6 ounces blue cheese

½ cup heavy cream

¼ teaspoon ground black pepper

PROCEDURE

Place the blue cheese, cream, and pepper in a food processor and blend until smooth.

TO FINISH

Split your baguette down the middle lengthwise. Smear one side with the creamy blue cheese and the other with bacon jam. Slice your venison steaks ⅛ inch thick and arrange the venison slices on the blue-cheese side of the baguette, slightly overlapping each one. Sandwich the baguette halves and slice into individual portions for serving.

BLACK AND BLUE GUT LOIN CARPACCIO
WITH GARLIC AIOLI

This isn't a true carpaccio because the meat isn't raw, but searing the gut loin, or tenderloin, gives it an extra layer of flavor. Sear it just enough to get a rich color on the exterior, and then chill the meat and slice it as thinly as possible against the grain. It tastes great alone as an appetizer but could be served as a shared appetizer with a grilled baguette.

GUT LOIN CARPACCIO

INGREDIENTS

1 venison gut loin

Kosher salt

Ground black pepper

2 lemons

4 tablespoons pickled beets from your favorite pickle maker, diced

2 tablespoons capers, rinsed and drained

8 sprigs tarragon, leaves stripped from the stems

4-inch knob fresh horseradish

PROCEDURE

Heat a cast-iron pan over medium-high until hot. Season the loin with salt and pepper, and then sear it on all sides until medium rare. Let the meat rest for 10 minutes, then tightly wrap the loin in plastic wrap and store it in the refrigerator until chilled through. Once chilled, slice it into rounds as thinly as humanly possible. A meat slicer works best here, but a sharp knife and a skilled hand will do the job as well.

GARLIC AIOLI

INGREDIENTS

2 small cloves garlic, mashed to paste

1 teaspoon fresh lemon juice, plus additional to taste

⅛ teaspoon kosher salt

½ cup mayonnaise

PROCEDURE

In a food processor, combine the mashed garlic, lemon juice, salt, and mayonnaise until emulsified. Add additional lemon juice and salt to taste.

TO FINISH

Lay the thin slices of meat over a couple of plates, but do not place the slices directly on top of each other. Slice the lemons into wedges and squeeze them evenly over all the slices. Garnish with the diced pickled beets, capers, and tarragon leaves. Put the aioli into a squeeze bottle and dot the empty spaces of the plates with 7 to 8 small dollops. Finish the plates by using a microplane grater to grate fresh horseradish to taste over everything. Season with a little salt and pepper.

To make this dish well, the venison has to be cut paper thin. Doing this will give it a nice texture and also allow the acid in the lemon juice to just barely begin to "cook" it.

Roasted Shoulder, Seasoned Ricotta, and Chilled Asparagus Salad
with Champagne Vinaigrette

To develop as much flavor as possible on this trussed cut, you want to get a solid sear, as dark as possible, on all sides of the meat before it hits the oven to roast. Searing in a cast-iron pan will give the best results. After you achieve a rich color on all sides of the meat, roasting it in a low-temperature oven until it's medium rare will help tenderize the usually chewy cut. Once it's cooled, slice it as thinly as possible against the grain to help maximize tenderness.

ROASTED SHOULDER

INGREDIENTS

1 shoulder cut (1½ to 2 pounds)

Grapeseed oil

Kosher salt

PROCEDURE

Usually when dealing with a larger cut from the shoulder, you won't have a super-symmetrical piece of meat to sear and cook, which is where trussing comes into play. There are a couple of ways to truss a piece of meat, but it's a skill that's hard to learn unless someone is teaching you live. Jacques Pépin's incredible book *La Technique* has a good guide to trussing. He also has some helpful online tutorials. Another option is to just cut pieces of butcher's twine and tie them like shoelaces firmly down the length of the steak, about an inch apart from each other, to make the meat more uniform (see page 78).

Preheat the oven to 250°F (121°C). Coat the bottom of a cast-iron pan with grapeseed oil and set on medium-high heat until the oil just begins to smoke. Lightly and evenly season the trussed roast with salt and place it in the pan. As the sides begin to caramelize, rotate the meat until all sides are equally dark brown. Transfer the meat to a roasting pan with a resting rack and place it in oven. Cook until it hits an internal temperature of 130°F (55°C), about 45 minutes or so depending on the size of the roast. Remove the meat from the oven and let it cool to room temperature. Wrap it tightly with plastic wrap and place it in your refrigerator until it's completely chilled, 6 to 7 hours. Immediately before serving, slice it very thinly against the grain and set aside.

Trussing is a handy skill when dealing with an asymmetrical cut of meat. It's also a difficult skill to learn without a one-on-one tutorial. Once you pick it up, you'll be able to do it with a single length of butcher's twine, as shown in this photo sequence. In the meantime, a simpler option is to use several equal lengths of twine spaced about an inch apart down the length of the cut.

SEASONED RICOTTA

INGREDIENTS

1 cup whole-milk ricotta

1 tablespoon capers, rinsed and drained

1 anchovy, minced

2 teaspoons honey

1 teaspoon minced flat-leaf parsley

Kosher salt

Ground black pepper

PROCEDURE

In a mixing bowl, combine the ricotta, capers, anchovy, honey, and parsley with a rubber spatula or spoon. Add salt and pepper to taste and chill until needed.

CHILLED ASPARAGUS SALAD

INGREDIENTS

1 bunch asparagus, ends trimmed

5 breakfast radishes, thinly sliced on a mandolin

PROCEDURE

Bring a pot (large enough to fit the asparagus into it) of salted water to a boil. While the water is coming to a boil, prepare an ice-water bath by filling a large bowl with water and adding several handfuls of ice. Once the water is boiling, blanch the asparagus for 20 to 30 seconds so that the asparagus has brightened and is slightly cooked but still crisp. Remove the asparagus and dunk it into the ice-water bath until it's fully chilled. Remove the asparagus from the water bath and slice them on the bias into small, bite-sized pieces.

CHAMPAGNE VINAIGRETTE

INGREDIENTS

1 shallot, finely minced

2 tablespoons champagne vinegar

¼ teaspoon kosher salt

½ teaspoon ground black pepper

½ cup grapeseed oil

Aged Parmesan cheese, for serving

PROCEDURE

Whisk together the shallot, vinegar, salt, and pepper. Add the grapeseed oil and whisk the vinaigrette until it's emulsified. Add additional salt to taste. If preparing the vinaigrette ahead of time, whisk it again before serving.

TO FINISH

Combine the sliced asparagus, sliced radishes, and enough vinaigrette to lightly coat the vegetables in a mixing bowl and set aside. Salt to taste.

With a spoon, spread the seasoned ricotta on the bottom of a large plate. Shingle slices of the venison over the ricotta, and lay the asparagus salad over the slices of venison. Grate Parmesan over the entire plate (be generous!) and drizzle a little more vinaigrette over the plate as well. Add extra salt and pepper as needed and serve. This also goes very well on top of toasted baguette.

FARRO AND BRUSSELS SPROUTS SOUP
WITH VENISON LEG

The feeling of coming in from the cold to a steaming-hot, hearty bowl of soup is hard to beat. This soup fits that objective perfectly. I recommend it after a long morning of freezing in the deer stand. The porcini adds a bit of extra savor that makes it stand out from other brothy soups.

INGREDIENTS

1 tablespoon grapeseed oil

2 pounds venison leg, diced into ½-inch cubes

2 onions, thinly sliced

3 medium carrots, thinly sliced

5 small celery ribs, thinly sliced

4 cloves garlic, thinly sliced

Kosher salt

½ cup dried porcini mushroom powder

1½ cups farro, rinsed with warm water

2 quarts Bone Broth (see page 56) or chicken stock

3 bay leaves

1 quart brussels sprouts, quartered

Ground black pepper

Freshly squeezed lemon juice

PROCEDURE

Heat a stock pot on the stove until it's just smoking, add the grapeseed oil, and place the diced venison into the pot in small batches so that it's not overcrowded and the meat can develop some colors. As soon as the venison is browned on one side, remove it from the pan and set it aside on a plate for later. This step may take three or four rounds, depending on the size of your pan. Next, add the onions, carrots, celery, garlic, and a pinch of salt and cook until translucent, about 10 minutes. Add the dried mushroom powder and farro and lightly toast in the pan about 2 minutes, being careful not to burn it. Add bone broth or chicken stock to liberally cover the farro and let simmer with the bay leaves until the farro is tender, about 40 minutes. Add the brussels sprouts and simmer until they begin to soften, about 10–15 minutes. Then add the venison back to the pot and let simmer for 2 minutes or until the venison is warmed again but still not cooked all the way through.

VENISON NECK SPLIT PEA SOUP

A lot of flavor can be extracted from the venison neck by slowly simmering it in a soup base until the meat easily falls off. It's best to simmer this soup with a lid on the pot and occasionally rotate the neck so that each side spends an equal amount of time fully submerged in liquid. Depending on how hot your stove is, you will have to add differing amounts of bone broth, so keep a generous supply nearby.

INGREDIENTS

1 tablespoon butter

4 cups small-diced yellow onion

1 cup small-diced carrot

1 cup small-diced celery

2 cloves garlic, sliced

1 tablespoon fresh thyme, minced

1 cup diced fennel

1 cup sliced leeks

2 teaspoons kosher salt

1 tablespoon red pepper flakes

5 quarts Bone Broth (see page 56) or chicken stock, plus more as needed

1 venison neck

1½ cups yellow split peas

½ cup heavy cream

1 pound roughly chopped spinach

Crème fraîche, for serving

Minced chives, for serving

PROCEDURE

In a large soup pot over medium-low heat, melt the butter and add the onion, carrot, celery, garlic, thyme, fennel, leeks, salt, and red pepper flakes. Continue to cook over medium low until the vegetables begin to soften and the onions appear slightly translucent, about 5 minutes. Add 5 quarts bone broth and the neck to the pot and simmer for about 3 hours. If the neck is not covered by liquid, continue to periodically flip it to encourage even cooking. Rinse the split peas and pick out any pebbles or off-looking peas. When the meat on the neck is tender, remove the neck from the pot and add the peas, then bring the soup back to a simmer. Meanwhile, pull off all the meat from the neck and finely chop it. When the peas are tender, after about 40 minutes, add the meat and cream to the soup. Bring the soup back up a soft simmer before adding in the spinach, then remove from the heat.

TO FINISH

Add more bone broth until the soup is at your desired consistency. Ladle into bowls and garnish with a dollop of crème fraîche and some minced chives.

VENISON AND PINEAPPLE CHILI

There's no shortage of opinions on what constitutes "real" chili. Some are full of beans or even noodles, while the more straightforward versions stick to meat, tomatoes, spices, and beer. This chili is in a league of its own with pineapple as one of its primary flavors—which I'm positive would make chili purists roll in their graves.

INGREDIENTS

2 pounds ground venison shoulder

3 tablespoons butter

3 poblano peppers, small diced

2 yellow onions, small diced

2 jalapeños, small diced

2 leeks, thinly sliced

2 cloves garlic, minced

½ pineapple, cleaned, cored and diced small (about 12 ounces)

2 tablespoons packed brown sugar

1 tablespoon tomato paste

1 teaspoon kosher salt

¼ cup chili powder

2 tablespoons ground cumin

2 tablespoons smoked paprika

2 (14.5-ounce) cans diced fire-roasted tomatoes

24 ounces pilsner

1 (15-ounce) can garbanzo beans, drained

8 ounces grated cheddar cheese, for serving

½ cup chopped fresh cilantro, for serving

PROCEDURE

Heat a soup pot over medium-high until hot, add enough grapeseed oil to cover the bottom of the pot and then sear the venison hard on one side. Stir to break up the meat and cook on all sides, then remove the meat and set aside. Reduce the heat to medium. Melt the butter in the pot and add the poblanos, onions, jalapeños, and leeks. Sauté until the vegetables have softened and the onions appear slightly translucent, about 5 minutes. Add the garlic, stir for just 30 seconds, then add the pineapple, brown sugar, tomato paste, and salt; stir occasionally. This mixture should take on a glaze-like consistency. When this happens, add back in the meat, chili powder, cumin, paprika, tomatoes, pilsner, and garbanzo beans. Bring the chili to a soft simmer for 10 minutes before serving.

TO FINISH

Ladle into bowls and garnish with grated cheddar cheese and cilantro.

ENTRÉES

I LOVE WHEN A BIG, HEAPING, DELICIOUS PLATE OF FOOD IS SET IN FRONT OF ME. IT'S ONE OF THE MOST ENJOYABLE FEELINGS. THESE RECIPES CREATE THAT FEELING AND ARE GREAT SERVED WITH AN ICE-COLD BEER OR TWO. SOME OF THESE TECHNIQUES MIGHT BE NEW TO YOU, SO DON'T EXPECT PERFECTION ON THE FIRST GO-ROUND. GIVE IT A FEW TRIES AND SEE WHAT WORKS BEST FOR YOU AND YOUR GUESTS.

Breakfast Sausage
with over-easy eggs and bacon brussels

After the meat is mixed, you'll need to bind the proteins by whipping them together by
hand or in a stand mixer. This process is called primary binding and helps the sausage
stick together, preventing a crumbly sausage. This recipe makes 2 pounds of loose
sausage that can be shaped into patties and frozen with small squares of parchment
paper separating the sausages. After that, wrap them in plastic in packs of two or three,
which will make it easy to pull the patties as needed. Brussels sprouts cooked with
bacon make for an interesting breakfast side and double down on the helping of pork
products—which is much appreciated in most circles.

BACON BRUSSELS

INGREDIENTS

4 strips bacon, cut into lardons

15 medium-sized brussels sprouts, cut in half the long way

Kosher salt to taste

Freshly squeezed lemon juice to taste

PROCEDURE

Place the bacon lardons into a pan that has a lot of surface area and place the pan onto a burner on medium heat. Cook the bacon until it's just beginning to get crispy, then remove it from the pan with a slotted spoon and set aside. Leave the rendered bacon fat in the pan. Place the halved brussels sprouts cut-side down into the pan and cook them until they are evenly browned and softened and they can be just pierced with a paring knife with little resistance. They may soak up all the bacon fat in this step—if so, add a little grapeseed oil so they're not cooking in a dry pan. Once they're cooked through, season with salt and stir the bacon back into the pan. Warm gently and add lemon juice to taste.

BREAKFAST SAUSAGE

INGREDIENTS

1 pound ground venison shoulder

1 pound ground pork belly

2 teaspoons kosher salt

2 teaspoons freshly cracked
black pepper

1 teaspoon brown sugar

1 teaspoon minced fresh sage

1 teaspoon minced fresh oregano

1 teaspoon red pepper flakes

½ teaspoon ground allspice

PROCEDURE

Add all the ingredients to a large mixing bowl or the bowl of a
stand mixer. If using a mixing bowl, massage the ingredients
together for about 5 minutes to create a primary bind. If using
a stand mixer, fit the mixer with the dough hook and spin it on
medium speed for 2 to 3 minutes, or until the meat starts to stick
together. Make small patties out of the sausage. Heat up a cast-iron
pan and place enough grapeseed oil in the pan to coat the bottom.
When it starts to smoke, add the sausage patties and sear on both
sides until they're cooked through.

OVER-EASY EGGS

INGREDIENTS

Two eggs per serving

Enough melted butter to coat the
bottom of the pan

Kosher salt

PROCEDURE

Melt the butter in a nonstick frying pan on medium heat. Once the
butter is bubbly, crack the eggs into the pan and let them cook until
the egg whites turn from translucent to solid white. Flip the eggs
and briefly cook on the other side until the eggs whites are set but
the yolk is still runny. Remove from the pan with a slotted spoon so
the excess butter drains off and flip once again onto a plate. Season
with kosher salt.

TO FINISH

Plate the sausage patties, eggs, and brussels sprouts.

BISCUITS
WITH COUNTRY-STYLE VENISON SAUSAGE GRAVY

≫——→ · ←——≪

When I first began cooking, I worked at a breakfast joint in Bozeman, Montana, where we served biscuits and gravy by the truckload. We'd make fresh biscuits every morning, and on most days, we'd run out by one or two o'clock in the afternoon. The owner and chef of the Cateye Cafe, Kevin Caracciolo, is still there making biscuits and gravy by hand every morning. Thankfully, he was willing to share his secret biscuit recipe for this book. If you're ever in Bozeman, stop in, ask for Kevlar, and tell him Jonny says "hi." I guarantee he'll give you a good reply.

VENISON SAUSAGE GRAVY

INGREDIENTS

1 pound venison breakfast sausage (recipe on page 94)

½ teaspoon dried fennel seed

1 teaspoon ground black pepper

1 tablespoon minced fresh sage

⅓ cup all-purpose flour

3 cups whole milk, plus more as needed

12 dashes Tabasco hot sauce, plus more to taste

PROCEDURE

Heat a large skillet or pan over medium-high heat. When it's hot, add the sausage in one giant patty that covers the entire bottom of the pan, then reduce the heat to medium. Let the fat render and the protein get a bit brown and crispy. Once the meat is brown, begin to stir it and break it into chunks, but keep the chunks fairly large. Cook until the sausage is just cooked through. Add the fennel, sage, black pepper, and flour. Turn the heat down to medium-low and stir continuously until the flour has turned golden and absorbed the fats, about 10 minutes. Whisk in the milk and Tabasco and bring to a soft simmer. Taste and add more salt, milk, and Tabasco as needed until the desired flavor and consistency is reached.

BISCUITS

INGREDIENTS

4 cups all-purpose flour

1 tablespoon plus 1 teaspoon baking powder

½ tablespoon plus ½ teaspoon kosher salt

½ teaspoon baking soda

3¾ ounces shortening, such as Crisco

1½ cups buttermilk

PROCEDURE

Preheat the oven to 350°F (177°C). Mix the flour, baking powder, salt, and baking soda in a large mixing bowl. Cut in the shortening with a fork until the dough resembles coarse crumbs. Add in the buttermilk and work the mass into a ball, but don't overknead the dough or it will become chewy. Using your hands, form eight or nine 4-ounce biscuits. Place the biscuits on a parchment-paper-lined baking sheet, and bake for 17 minutes or until they're golden brown on top and cooked through

TO FINISH

For each plate, split a biscuit and smother with gravy.

SAUSAGE BRAISE
WITH SAUERKRAUT AND BONE BROTH

I enjoy cooking family-style meals because they usually dirty fewer dishes and make for a great presentation at a table. Dropping a big plate of various meats, sauerkraut, and potatoes is bound to please even your toughest critics. A lot of hunters end up with some cased venison sausages and salami from the butcher who processed their meat; this recipe assumes that you have some in your freezer. Any sausage or salami will do here, but a Weisswurst or bratwurst will work exceptionally well with this dish.

INGREDIENTS

⅔ cup small-diced salami, casing removed (about 5 ounces)

2 tablespoons butter

2 yellow onions, diced

1 clove garlic, minced

1 tablespoon minced fresh thyme

1 cup white wine

1 32-ounce jar good sauerkraut

1 quart Bone Broth (see page 56) or chicken stock

1 pound fingerling potatoes

4 smoked venison sausages

2 tablespoons butter, cold

Kosher salt to taste

2 tablespoons chopped parsley

PROCEDURE

Heat a large heavy-bottomed pan or pot over medium heat. When the pan is hot, sear the salami, stirring occasionally to brown all sides. Remove the salami from the pan, and then add the first 2 tablespoons butter to the empty pan. When the butter melts, add the onions, garlic, and thyme to the pan and cook until the onions appear slightly translucent, about 5 minutes. Add the white wine, sauerkraut, and bone broth; simmer until the liquid has reduced to three-quarters of the original volume, about 10 minutes. Separately, boil the fingerling potatoes in well-salted water until tender, about 25 minutes. Drain the potatoes. When they are cool enough to handle, cut them into bite-sized pieces on the bias. In a medium-high-heat sauté pan or on the grill, sear the sausages until the casing is browned. Add the potatoes, salami, sausages, kraut, and bone broth to the pan and continue simmering until everything is hot and the broth has a stew-like consistency. Melt in the butter, season with salt to taste, and then add the parsley.

TO FINISH
Pour the contents of the pan onto a large plate and serve family style.

SCHNITZEL
WITH CREAMY KALE AND GRILLED LEMONS

≫———→ • ←———≪

Schnitzel is a great use for larger, leaner cuts of meat. Slicing the venison against the grain and using a meat mallet to pound it out makes for a very tender bite. The fast cooking process also helps avoid overcooking—just cook the breading until it's golden brown on both sides and serve immediately. The creamy kale has the potential to get a little runny here, so make sure that the blanched leaves are squeezed thoroughly of any excess moisture before they're added to the cream.

SCHNITZEL

INGREDIENTS

4 venison hindquarter portions, thinly sliced

1 cup all-purpose flour

5 eggs, beaten

1 cup panko breadcrumbs

Kosher salt

Grapeseed oil

PROCEDURE

To pound the venison, place the venison slices in between 2 sheets of plastic wrap on a sturdy work surface and gently pound the meat out until it's about ⅛ inch thick throughout. A meat mallet works best, but if you don't have one, just grab a rolling pin or wine bottle and have at it. Try your best to get an even piece of venison to ensure an evenly cooked end result. Once you have your meat to your desired thickness, set up three shallow bowls and use one for the flour, one for the eggs, and one for the panko. Set your bowls next to each other in the order of flour, eggs, and panko. Lightly salt each side of the venison slices. Working with one slice at a time, place a slice in the flour bowl and coat it. Shake off any extra flour and dip the venison into the egg bowl, and then dip it into the panko bowl, making sure it's fully covered with breadcrumbs. Transfer the breaded slice to a plate and repeat the process with all of the slices, stacking them on the plate.

To fry, heat a well-seasoned cast-iron pan over medium-high heat heat. Add grapeseed oil to about a ⅛-inch depth and fry the breaded venison quickly on one side until it's lightly browned, then flip and fry the other side until lightly browned. Remove from the pan to a paper-towel-lined plate and pat dry.

CREAMY KALE

INGREDIENTS

2 pounds kale, chopped with stems removed

4 tablespoons butter

1 yellow onion, julienned

2 cloves garlic, thinly sliced

2 jalapeños, diced

¼ cup all-purpose flour

1 cup heavy cream

Kosher salt

Juice from Grilled Lemons, to taste (see 107)

PROCEDURE

Prepare an ice bath. Place two cups of ice in a large mixing bowl and add enough cold water to cover the ice by 2–3 inches. Next, bring a large pot of salted water to a boil. Drop your chopped kale into the pot and let it simmer for a minute or so. With a large slotted spoon, remove the kale and place it in a colander with a handle and dunk into the ice bath. Once cooled, drain the kale, squeeze all the excess liquid out of the kale, and set it aside. Separately, in a large stockpot over medium heat, melt the butter. Add the onion, garlic, and jalapeños and sauté until they're tender, about 6 minutes. Sprinkle the flour into the pot, turn the heat to medium low and cook until it just starts to brown, making sure that it only slightly turns color, about 7 minutes. Whisk in the cream and let simmer until the sauce thickens, the flour is fully incorporated, and the sauce is reduced by half, about 5 minutes. Add the kale to the sauce and season with salt and grilled lemon juice to taste.

GRILLED LEMONS

INGREDIENTS

2 lemons

PROCEDURE

Cut the lemons across their equators. On a hot grill, grill the lemons cut-side down until nice char lines have developed.

Grilled lemons are a great way to add a more developed citrus flavor to any dish. Keep a few of these on hand in your fridge to squeeze over salads and fish or to use in vinaigrette.

TO FINISH

Spoon the creamy kale on the bottom of each plate and lean a piece of schnitzel against the kale. Serve with a grilled lemon and squeeze on as desired.

Raw Kale Salad
with leg paillard and garlic, anchovy, and herb vinaigrette

This is another one of those everyday dishes that I could eat over and over and never get sick of. The kale is softened only by acidity from the lemons and salt, and by massaging it, so make sure it's chopped into small bite-sized pieces for easy eating. The venison is prepared in a fashion similar to the schnitzel (see page 103). Pounding the venison has two purposes: it helps tenderize the meat, and it allows for a shorter cooking time, which ultimately retains more moisture. Rather than breading the venison, just lightly fry it in a pan with grapeseed oil.

GARLIC, ANCHOVY, AND HERB VINAIGRETTE

INGREDIENTS

1 tablespoon shallot, finely minced

1 garlic clove, finely minced

1 anchovy filet, cleaned and finely minced

1 tablespoon Dijon mustard

3 tablespoons freshly-squeezed lemon juice

3 tablespoons fresh parsley, finely minced

½ cup grapeseed oil

¼ teaspoon kosher salt

½ teaspoon ground black pepper

PROCEDURE

In a small bowl, cover the shallot, garlic, anchovy, and mustard with lemon juice. In a second small bowl, cover the parsley with grapeseed oil. Rest both for 30 minutes. Whisk the two together with salt and pepper. Add salt, pepper, and/or lemon juice to taste. Cover and use within 30 minutes so the herbs don't brown. Whisk again before serving.

RAW KALE SALAD

INGREDIENTS

2 small bunches (12 ounces) curly kale, ribs removed and julienned into ⅛-inch ribbons

½ teaspoon kosher salt

1 teaspoon freshly squeezed lemon juice

½ cup freshly grated aged Parmesan cheese

½ cup toasted pine nuts

½ cup toasted slivered almonds

PROCEDURE

In a large bowl, mix the kale, salt, and the lemon juice. Massage it 2–3 minutes to help soften.

VENISON PAILLARD

INGREDIENTS

4 venison leg steaks, each about 5 ounces

Grapeseed oil to coat a pan

Kosher salt

Ground black pepper

PROCEDURE

Place the venison steaks one at a time on a cutting board and cover with plastic wrap. Using a meat mallet or a wine bottle, pound the steaks into a ¼-inch thickness. Season with salt and pepper. On the stovetop, warm to medium heat a pan large enough to fit the steaks and just enough grapeseed oil to coat the pan. Lay the steaks in and gently warm until one side is cooked halfway through, trying to avoid a lot of browning. Flip and repeat. When the steaks are cooked to medium, about 4 minutes each side, remove from the pan, thinly slice, and set aside.

TO FINISH

Coat the salad with ¾ of the vinaigrette and toss, massaging one last time to soften the kale further. Place a serving of kale in a bowl. On a plate, drizzle remaining vinaigrette over the venison and then place a sliced steak on top of the kale. Finish with a small handful of toasted pine nuts and almonds and a healthy dose of freshly grated Parmesan.

SMOKED LEG STEAK
WITH COLESLAW

In my home, smoked meats can typically be found at the ready in the fridge for any meal. Having a stash lying around is a good way to take salads, sandwiches, breakfasts, and countless other meals to another level. And although the leftovers of this meal will be great, one of my favorite things to snack on are meats directly out of the smoker next to a big pile of vinegary coleslaw. Smoke, meat, and slaw go together as well as anything.

This smoke is meant to be made from a larger leg muscle, particularly the eye of round, but other large muscles in the leg will do as well. Once the muscles in the leg are trimmed up, they come out fairly lean without a lot of connective tissue holding them together, so a low smoke until the meat hits 130°–140°F (55°–60°C) will suffice. I smoke leaner cuts like this over a water bath, which creates a gentler cooking atmosphere. I like to use an apple or pecan wood for a stronger flavor with less time in the smoker. This rib rub recipe makes way more than you'll need, so save the extra for your next smoke.

SMOKED LEG STEAK

INGREDIENTS

2–3 pounds venison leg muscle

Rib Rub (see page 72)

PROCEDURE

Rub the rib rub evenly over the entire muscle. Place the muscle onto a rack in your smoker and place a water bath on another rack directly underneath the leg muscle. Heat the smoker to 225°F (107°C) with either apple or pecan wood and cook until the muscle reaches an internal temperature of 130°–140°F (55°– 60°C). Remove the meat from the smoker and let it rest.

COLESLAW

INGREDIENTS

1½ cups apple cider vinegar

½ cup granulated sugar

2 tablespoons kosher salt

1 teaspoon ground black pepper

1½ pounds red cabbage, thinly shredded

7 ounces kale, ribs removed and thinly shredded

2 tablespoons toasted sesame seeds

PROCEDURE

Boil the vinegar, sugar, salt, and pepper in a saucepan over high heat. Set aside to cool. Mix the cabbage, kale, and sesame seeds in a large mixing bowl and pour the cooled dressing over the shredded vegetables until they're fully coated in vinegar mix. Toss and let sit 5 minutes before serving. Toss once again immediately before serving.

TO FINISH

Slice the smoked meat against the grain, about ½ inch thick and shingle the slices on each plate next to a large pile of coleslaw.

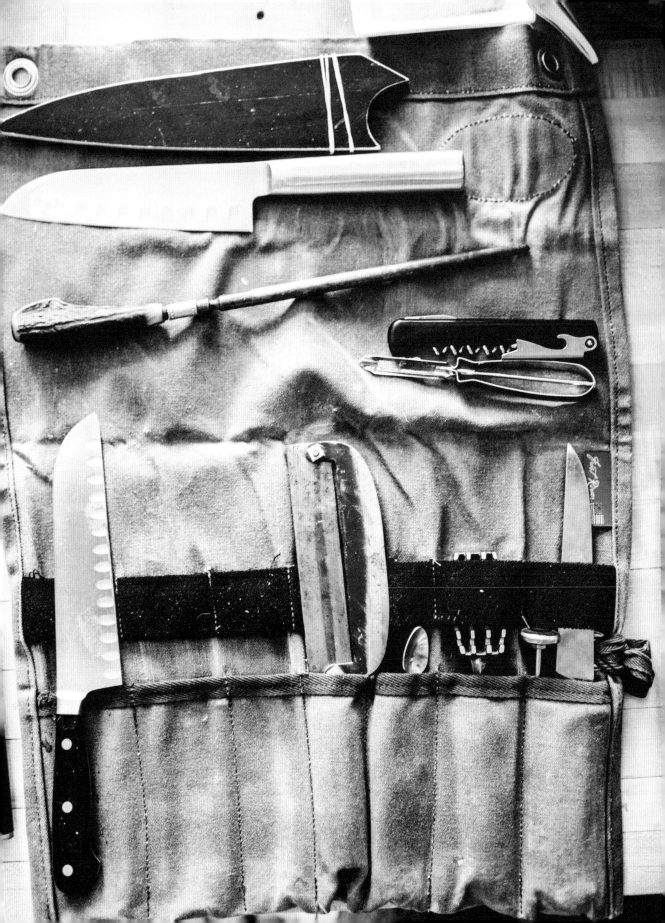

BURGERS
WITH SWEET POTATO FRIES AND CHIMICHURRI

This is another dish that can benefit from mixing ground pork shoulder with the venison. I didn't write it that way here, but if you have kids or someone at the table who doesn't like a strong game flavor, substituting up to half the venison with ground pork shoulder will reduce the gamey flavor and help keep the burger moist. Melting a soft Camembert or brie on the burger adds some needed richness, and serving it on a toasted English muffin really lets the burger shine through. To increase efficiency, start the fries first—by the time they are done, you should be able to complete the rest of the meal. If you really want to crank it up, add Bacon Jam (page 69).

BURGERS

INGREDIENTS

1½ pound ground venison shoulder

Kosher salt

Ground black pepper

2 tablespoons grapeseed oil

8 ounces Camembert (or a soft brie)

4 English muffins, split, buttered, and toasted

PROCEDURE

Preheat oven to 400°F (204°C). Divide the ground venison into 4 6-ounce portions, then pat each one into a ½-inch-thick patty. Salt and pepper both sides of the patties. Heat a cast-iron pan with just enough grapeseed oil to cover the bottom of the pan. When the pan is evenly hot, sear the burgers on one side until a nice crust has formed. Flip the burgers and immediately add 2 ounces of cheese to each burger. Transfer the pan to the oven for 5 minutes or until your desired doneness is reached. Serve immediately.

SWEET POTATO FRIES

INGREDIENTS

3 medium sweet potatoes

2 tablespoons grapeseed oil
(enough to coat the fries)

Kosher salt

Ground black pepper

PROCEDURE

Preheat the oven to 400°F (204°C). Cut each potato into 8 long
wedges, then toss with grapeseed oil to lightly coat the wedges.
Season them with salt and pepper, and arrange the wedges on a
rimmed baking sheet skin-side down. Roast for 20 minutes, or until
the wedges are fork-tender and the edges have just begun to brown.

CHIMICHURRI

INGREDIENTS

1 cup firmly packed whole-leaf
parsley, chopped

2 tablespoons chopped fresh
oregano

1 clove garlic, finely minced

1 tablespoon champagne vinegar

1 tablespoon freshly squeezed
lime juice

½ cup grapeseed oil

¼ teaspoon red pepper flakes

Kosher salt

PROCEDURE

In a medium bowl, combine the parsley, oregano, and garlic. Add the
vinegar, lime juice, grapeseed oil, and red pepper flakes; whisk with
a spoon until well combined. Add salt to taste.

TO FINISH

Put each burger in a split English muffin and put it onto a plate.
Add sweet potato fries to each plate as well and drizzle the fries
with chimichurri.

TACOS
WITH JOSIE'S PICO DE GALLO, FENNEL CABBAGE SLAW, AND GARLIC AIOLI

≫⟶ · ⟵≪

Tacos are one food that have stayed in my diet throughout my life. From late-night Taco Bell runs in my earlier years until now, when a good taco is the best meal of the week, they've always been there for me. Nowadays I serve my tacos on a fresh-grilled corn tortilla with a little bit of ground, chopped, or braised meat and an array of fresh accoutrements on the table. I like a variety of fresh items—something spicy, something acidic, something fatty, and something crisp. We get touches of all those things here, mixed into the slaw and the pico, but feel free to add more ingredients to your table— it will only add to the meal. This pico de gallo recipe has a special place in my heart because one of my former prep cooks, Josie, used to make it for our kitchen at lunch. Everyone always raved about it. Now you get to as well.

TACOS

INGREDIENTS

Grapeseed oil

1½ pounds ground venison

2 tablespoons Blackening Mix (see page 135)

¼ cup Bone Broth (see page 56), chicken broth, or beer

32 small corn tortillas (two per taco)

Garlic Aioli (see page 75), for serving

PROCEDURE

Heat a large stainless-steel sauté pan over high heat. Pour enough oil in the pan to coat the bottom. In one flat layer, add the ground venison to the pan. Keep the heat on high and let the venison brown on one side. Turn the heat down to medium and chop the venison up with a spoon until it looks like ground taco meat. Add the spice mix and cook until the meat is cooked all the way through. Skim off any excessive fat, turn the heat to low, and add the bone broth. Let it simmer for 5 minutes, or until the taco meat has absorbed the liquid. Taste for seasoning and set aside.

JOSIE'S PICO DE GALLO

INGREDIENTS

3 small tomatoes, chopped

½ cup small-diced yellow onion

½ jalapeño, finely minced

½ English cucumber, peeled and diced small

Juice of half a lime

¼ cup chopped cilantro

4 teaspoons kosher salt

PROCEDURE

Combine the tomatoes, onion, jalapeño, and cucumber in a mixing bowl, then add the lime juice. Right before serving, add the cilantro and season with salt to taste.

FENNEL CABBAGE SLAW

INGREDIENTS

1 pound red cabbage, thinly sliced

1 fennel bulb, thinly sliced

1 teaspoon salt

Juice of half a lemon

2 teaspoons honey

½ cup Garlic Aioli (see page 75)

PROCEDURE

Place the cabbage and fennel in a mixing bowl with the salt and lemon juice. With your hands, rub the salt and lemon into the vegetables for about 2 minutes to soften them. Pour off any excess liquid, then add the honey and aioli and toss. Add more salt and lemon if desired.

TO FINISH

Grill the corn tortillas and wrap them in a cloth towel. Set the tortillas and your other accoutrements on the table and let your guests dig in. I recommend two tortillas per taco.

Meatloaf
WITH EMBER-ROASTED ROOT VEGETABLES AND BOURBON-MAPLE BUTTER

Meatloaf has the potential to be an all-star or a dud. I wanted to step away from serving it with ketchup and mashed potatoes but not end up so far removed that it didn't still feel like a homey dish. I first learned to make ember-roasted root vegetables at The Bachelor Farmer in Minneapolis, Minnesota, where we utilized the fireplaces as much as possible. Their chef and my friend, Paul Berglund, was very skilled at finding ways to leverage the tools he had around him to enhance our cooking, and this was one of those techniques. The root vegetables are thrown directly into hot coals and then turned occasionally so that they blacken evenly on all sides until they're soft in the middle. The charring creates an interesting flavor profile, and the hardened charred skins trap the moisture and amplify the vegetables' naturally occurring sweetness.

VENISON MEATLOAF

INGREDIENTS

1 cup milk

3 cups sourdough, diced (no crusts)

1 pound ground venison shoulder

1 pound ground pork shoulder

1 pound ground beef

1 medium onion, finely diced

3 eggs, beaten

2 cups ricotta cheese

2 tablespoons fresh thyme leaves, chopped

2 tablespoons ground fennel seed

2 tablespoons chopped parsley

1 teaspoon Worcestershire sauce

1 tablespoon kosher salt

PROCEDURE

In a small mixing bowl, mix the bread and the milk. Let it soak for 20 minutes or until all the milk has absorbed into the bread. Preheat the oven to 350°F (177°C). Gently squeeze out any excess milk from the bread. In a larger mixing bowl, add all the remaining ingredients together with the soaked bread. With your hands, mix the ingredients together until they are fully incorporated, then continue to mix for another minute or two until the meat begins to stick to itself a little. Next, line a meatloaf-shaped baking dish with plastic wrap, using enough plastic wrap so it hangs over the edge of the pan by 6 inches on each side. Place the mixed meat on the plastic wrap and gently press it down until it's completely compact. Fold the plastic over the top of the meatloaf. Place the pan containing the meatloaf in a larger baking pan that comes at least three-quarters of the way up the sides of the meatloaf pan. Pour hot water into the larger pan until it reaches just over halfway up the wall of the meatloaf pan. Place in the oven and cook for about 1½ hours, or until the meatloaf reaches 155°F (68°C).

EMBER-ROASTED ROOT VEGETABLES

INGREDIENTS

2 pounds of root vegetables of your choice (I recommend rutabaga and/or turnips. Gourd vegetables like butternut squash or pumpkin work too.)

8 tablespoons butter, melted

2 cups whole milk

Kosher salt

PROCEDURE

This is a completely technique-based recipe that takes some finesse and does not have a replicable procedure, meaning it always changes based on the size of your vegetables and the temperature of the fire. Get a fire going in the fire pit or in the bottom of a grill with properly dried wood. Once the flames turn to coals, drop your vegetables directly on the coals. They will blacken, but you're going to be scraping off the layer of ash anyway, so don't be worried. Turn them occasionally so that they get an even amount of char all over. If the vegetables are extremely small, it may help to set them to the side of the ashes rather than directly on them. Cook them until they're knife-tender, 20–40 minutes, depending on the vegetable. Once they're ready, pull them off the fire and set aside until you can comfortably handle them. With a paring knife, peel the outside layer of hard ash off the vegetables and discard. Leave the secondary layer of blackened vegetable.

In a saucepan, warm the milk over low heat, add the butter to the milk and heat until the butter melts completely. Place the hot vegetables in a mixing bowl and slowly mix in the butter-and-milk mixture until the mash reaches your desired texture. Depending on the types of vegetables, you may not use all the mixture or you may need a bit more. Season with salt to taste.

Once cooked, remove the root vegetables and set them aside until you can handle them without burning yourself. The trick to peeling them is to use a paring knife to remove the extremely black and charred exterior.

BOURBON-MAPLE BUTTER

INGREDIENTS

4 tablespoons unsalted butter, very soft

1 tablespoon good-quality bourbon

1 tablespoon maple syrup

1 tablespoon minced chives

1 teaspoon salt

PROCEDURE

Combine all the ingredients in a food processor. Keep at room temperature so it remains soft.

TO FINISH

Remove the meatloaf from the plastic and slice. Plate each slice with a large spoonful of hot mashed root vegetables on top of the meatloaf, and dot the pile of root vegetables with a scoop of the butter.

CORI'S HOT DISH

Around the same time I opened my catering business, I was lucky enough to meet Cori, who's helped make my business run smoother and the food we serve significantly better. For her day job, she makes mountains of handmade sausages, and on weekends she shoots guns and rides motorcycles, making her a full-fledged badass. When she insisted that this book needed a good old-fashioned hot dish, I had no option but to oblige. This is her version.

INGREDIENTS

1½ pounds root vegetables (use a combination of your favorites, such as celery root, rutabaga, turnip, parsnip, and potato)

2 tablespoons grapeseed oil

1 pound ground venison shoulder

1 cup mushrooms, thinly sliced

¼ cup celery, small diced

½ cup carrot, small diced

1 cup yellow onion, small diced

4 cloves garlic, minced

2 tablespoons fresh thyme leaves, chopped

2 teaspoons fresh rosemary leaves, chopped

4 tablespoons butter

½ cup all-purpose flour

1 cup heavy cream

1 cup Bone Broth (see page 56) or chicken stock

1 teaspoon kosher salt

1½ teaspoons ground black pepper

½ cup raw wild rice, cooked

½ cup breadcrumbs

¾ cup shredded Parmesan cheese

PROCEDURE

Preheat the oven to 375° F (191° C). Cube the root vegetables into ½-inch pieces and toss with enough grapeseed oil to coat, about 2 tablespoons. Spread on a rimmed baking sheet and roast until you can just pierce them with a fork, about 20 minutes. Add just enough grapeseed oil to cover the bottom of a sauté pan and sear the venison, breaking it up into bite-sized pieces. Once some good color has developed, remove the meat from the pan and set it aside. Add more grapeseed oil if needed to just cover the bottom of the pan and add the rest of the vegetables. Mushrooms will release a good amount of moisture; when that has cooked off add the garlic, thyme, and rosemary and stir for 30 seconds. Add the butter to the pan and once it has melted add flour and stir periodically for 5 minutes. Next, whisk in the heavy cream and the broth or stock and cook until just thickened. Turn off heat. Stir in wild rice, venison, salt, and pepper. Spread the root vegetables in your baking dish and pour the rice and venison mixture over the root vegetables. Combine breadcrumbs and Parmesan and sprinkle over top of the hot dish. Bake for 20–30 minutes or until bubbly and a golden crust has developed.

BLACKENED SIRLOIN
WITH BLISTERED GREEN BEANS AND HERB VINAIGRETTE

Sirloin, which comes from the top front of the hindquarter, is a great cut for this recipe, but the recipe will work well with any leaner leg steak. Cover the steak in the blackening mix and give it a hard sear or grill it on all sides until it looks crisp and burnt. It's a great way to bring a lot of flavor to the plate, and serving it alongside blistered green beans doubles down on that char flavor—while the chimichurri freshens it back up.

INGREDIENTS

4 leg steaks

Blackening Mix (see page 135)

Grapeseed oil

PROCEDURE

Evenly coat the steaks with the blackening mix. In a hot pan with a layer of grapeseed oil over high heat or on a hot grill, cook the steaks, turning them to cook each side evenly, until they have a blackened look to them and reach an internal temperature of 130°F (54°C). Pull from the heat and let rest.

BLACKENING MIX

INGREDIENTS

3 tablespoons kosher salt

1 tablespoon smoked paprika

1 tablespoon ground white pepper

1 teaspoon garlic powder

1 teaspoon onion powder

1 teaspoon mustard powder

1 teaspoon dried oregano

1 teaspoon dried thyme leaves

PROCEDURE

Combine all the ingredients in a small bowl.

BLISTERED GREEN BEANS

INGREDIENTS

2 pounds green beans, trimmed

2 tablespoons grapeseed oil

Kosher salt

Ground black pepper

PROCEDURE

Heat a cast-iron pan over high heat. In a large mixing bowl, toss the green beans with the oil and season with salt and pepper. When the pan is rippin' hot (it may start to smoke), toss the green beans in the pan. Sear the green beans on one side until they begin to blacken and blister. Using tongs, reposition the green beans to sear the other side. Remove from the heat when the green beans have been blackened and blistered to your liking.

HERB VINAIGRETTE

INGREDIENTS

1 tablespoon finely minced shallot

3 tablespoons fresh lemon juice

3 tablespoons finely minced fresh parsley

1 tablespoon finely minced fresh thyme

½ cup grapeseed oil

¾ teaspoon kosher salt

¼ teaspoon ground black pepper

Lemon wedges, for serving

PROCEDURE

In a small bowl, cover the shallot with lemon juice and let rest for 30 minutes. In a second small bowl, cover the parsley and thyme with oil and let rest for 30 minutes. After 30 minutes, whisk together the two mixtures with the salt and pepper. Add additional salt, pepper, or lemon juice until the desired flavor is reached. (If prepared ahead of time, whisk the vinaigrette again before serving.)

TO FINISH

Slice the steaks against the grain and garnish with the herb vinaigrette. In a mixing bowl, combine the beans with enough herb vinaigrette to coat them evenly, but not so much that they're drowning in it. Plate the green beans alongside the steaks and finish with a squeeze of lemon, if desired.

Pan-Seared Loin
WITH WHOLE ROASTED CAULIFLOWER, CAULIFLOWER PURÉE, AND TOASTED BREADCRUMBS

I like this dish because it comes off as a little more refined than some of the other recipes in the book, and when the venison is cooked well, it has a stunning presentation. The venison is pan-roasted with all-purpose rub and served alongside cauliflower prepared two different ways: roasted whole and as a purée with a hit of vinegar and butter. The purée should come out a little thicker than a stew consistency, so depending on the size of the cauliflower head, adjust the amount of liquid you put into the pot. It's always easier to add more later than it is to take some away. The entire dish gets a splattering of herb-toasted breadcrumbs for texture and herbaceousness. When served on white plates, the white-on-white effect really makes the well-cooked venison backstrap or tenderloin pop.

PAN-SEARED LOIN

INGREDIENTS

1½ pounds whole venison loin

Rib Rub (see page 72)

Grapeseed oil

Olive oil, to finish

PROCEDURE

Heat a heavy-bottomed sauté pan over high heat. Add enough grapeseed oil to the pan to evenly coat the bottom. Lightly coat the loin with rib rub, and when the oil begins to smoke, lay the loin in the pan. Cook each side of the loin until it's browned evenly on all sides and has an internal temperature of 130°F (54°C). Remove the loin and set it aside to rest.

WHOLE ROASTED CAULIFLOWER

INGREDIENTS

1 head cauliflower, greens removed and trimmed so the cauliflower lays flat on its stem

Grapeseed oil

3 tablespoons butter

1 sprig fresh sage

1 sprig fresh rosemary

Kosher salt

PROCEDURE

Preheat your oven to 450°F (232°C). Place the head of cauliflower in a cast-iron pan and coat it with grapeseed oil on all sides. Season the cauliflower head with salt and place it in the oven for about 45 minutes, or until it begins to brown. Pull the cauliflower out of the oven, place the pan on a burner on medium heat, and add the butter and herbs to the pan. Let the butter melt, and once it starts to bubble, tip the pan toward yourself so the butter collects in a puddle. Using a deep spoon, baste the bubbling butter continually over the cauliflower to finish cooking (about 3 minutes). To test for doneness, pierce the cauliflower with a paring knife. When the knife can be removed with little or no resistance, it's done.

CAULIFLOWER PURÉE

INGREDIENTS

¾ medium-sized cauliflower head

3 cloves garlic

3 cups Bone Broth (see page 56) or chicken stock

1 cup milk

Kosher salt

1 tablespoon butter, cold

2 teaspoons champagne vinegar

PROCEDURE

Chop the cauliflower into small florets and place them in a small stockpot with the garlic, bone broth, milk, and a pinch of salt. Place the pot on the stove and bring it to a simmer; let it simmer until the cauliflower is completely soft and a quarter of the liquid has evaporated. Let it cool for 10 to 15 minutes, then pour the mixture into a blender with the butter and champagne vinegar. Purée the mix until it's smooth. Add additional vinegar, broth, and salt to taste. Transfer the seasoned purée back into a clean pot and re-warm it on the stove.

TOASTED BREADCRUMBS

INGREDIENTS

2 tablespoons butter

1 teaspoon finely minced fresh rosemary

1 teaspoon finely minced fresh thyme

1 cup fresh breadcrumbs (from about 6 slices of bread)

PROCEDURE

Melt the butter in a sauté pan over medium heat and add the rosemary and thyme. Sauté for about 2 minutes, then add the breadcrumbs and stir them around until they are golden brown and crispy, about 6 minutes. Once they are crisp, remove them from the pan and set them on a paper towel to collect the excess butter.

TO FINISH

Place a large dollop of the purée on each plate. Cut the roasted cauliflower into quarters from the top looking down. Plate each slice of cauliflower with brown side facing the edge of the plate and the core lying flat. Cut off two 3-ounce portions from the loin and place next to the purée, cut-side up. Give them a small sprinkle of rib rub to finish. Finally, give the entire plate a light dusting of breadcrumbs and pour a small amount of olive oil on the steaks.

Porcini-Encrusted Loin
WITH MASHED POTATOES, MEAT SAUCE, AND WINTER PICKLES

When cooking this venison, you want to get a nice crust on the loin, but you also want to avoid burning the porcini. Keep a close eye on the steaks and turn them as needed. Use a thermometer to check the temperature of the steaks—I like mine at about 125°F (52°C)—and then let them rest for 5 to 6 minutes before cutting into them. The meat sauce here is challenging, but it amplifies the savory content tenfold with its lip-smacking gooeyness. If there's no time to make it as written, reduce the 2 quarts of bone broth on the stovetop until about ¾ cup remains, at which point it should resemble a gravy.

Follow the recipe and instructions for Winter Pickles found on page 61.

PORCINI-ENCRUSTED LOIN

INGREDIENTS

⅓ cup dried porcini mushrooms

1 venison loin, split into 4 steaks

Kosher salt

Grapeseed oil

Winter Pickles (see page 61)

PROCEDURE

To make porcini powder, take one or two handfuls of dried porcini mushroom and run them through a spice grinder. Measure out ½ cup and set aside. Generously season the venison steaks with salt and then coat them with porcini powder. Heat a cast-iron pan over high heat. When it's smoking hot, add enough grapeseed oil to coat the bottom of the pan. Carefully place the venison steaks in the pan, making sure to get a good sear on all sides, cooking them until they're around 125°F (52°C) in the center. Pull the steaks off the heat and let rest for 6 minutes before slicing into them.

MASHED POTATOES

INGREDIENTS

2½ pounds baby red potatoes, rinsed of dirt

Kosher salt

6 tablespoons butter

½ cup heavy cream

PROCEDURE

Place your potatoes in a large pot and add enough cold water to cover them by 3 inches. Add 2 tablespoons salt and bring the potatoes to a low simmer. Cook them until they are knife-tender and just starting to fall apart. In a separate pot, heat the butter and the cream together until the butter is melted. Strain the potatoes and transfer them to a large mixing bowl. Pour the butter-and-cream mixture into the potatoes. Using a handheld potato masher, roughly mash them until all the butter and cream is incorporated. Do not overmix. Add salt to taste.

MEAT SAUCE

INGREDIENTS

4 cups chopped bones (2- to 3-inch pieces)

1 (750ml) bottle pinot noir

2 quarts Bone Broth (see page 56) or chicken stock, divided

PROCEDURE

Heat a wide, heavy-bottomed skillet with no oil over high heat. When the pan is hot, add the bones but do not stir, letting the bones brown on one side. When a layer of crust, also known as fond, has developed on the bottom of the pan, add half the bottle of wine. Scrape up the fond and reduce the liquid until a layer of fond develops again, about 15 minutes. Add the other half of the bottle, scrape up the fond, and reduce the liquid to a glaze consistency, about 15 minutes. Add 1 quart bone broth and reduce again to a glaze consistency, about 15 minutes. Add 1 more quart bone broth and reduce by half, about 15 minutes and then strain through a fine-mesh strainer and discard the bones.

TO FINISH

Plate each serving with a scoop of mashed potatoes and top with a steak. Ladle some meat sauce over the steak and garnish with some of the pickles.

LOMO AL TRAPO
WITH SEARED BOK CHOY
AND ANCHOVY BUTTER

I was introduced to this technique by my friend Alex Roberts, a remarkable chef and restaurateur in the Twin Cities. The dish literally translates as "tenderloin in a cloth," and Alex's version, made with beef tenderloin, is an absolute showstopper. I'm adapting it here to work with venison loin, but the outcome is the same: a talking piece at any party and a delicious recipe. The entire loin is wrapped in cotton and salt and placed on top of hot coals, which means you can't see what's happening to the loin while it's cooking. It takes a little trust and a couple practice rounds to get this recipe down, but once you do, you'll be going back to it again and again. After the loin comes off the coals, brush off any excess salt before serving it or you'll end up with a salt lick.

One key to a successful Lomo Al Trapo is the generous use of kosher salt . . . that, and trust in the cooking process, since you can't observe the meat.

LOMO AL TRAPO

INGREDIENTS

1 venison loin

2 two-pound boxes kosher salt

PROCEDURE

In a grill, get a pile of charcoal burning until the coals turn to embers. Line a cotton towel (one that you don't mind burning) with a ¼-inch layer of kosher salt and place the loin in the middle of the towel. Wrap each side of the towel around the loin, making sure that the salt covers the loin. Continue wrapping the towel around the loin until it resembles a burrito, and tie the towel down with a couple pieces of butcher's twine. Take the package and place it directly on top of hot coals for 6 minutes. Flip the package and let it sit on the coals for another 6 minutes. Pull the package from the coals and place it on a clean cutting board. With scissors, remove the string, and then unwrap the loin from the towel. With a pastry brush, remove any excess salt from the loin and place the loin onto another clean cutting board. Let it rest for 7 minutes, then cut steaks out of it.

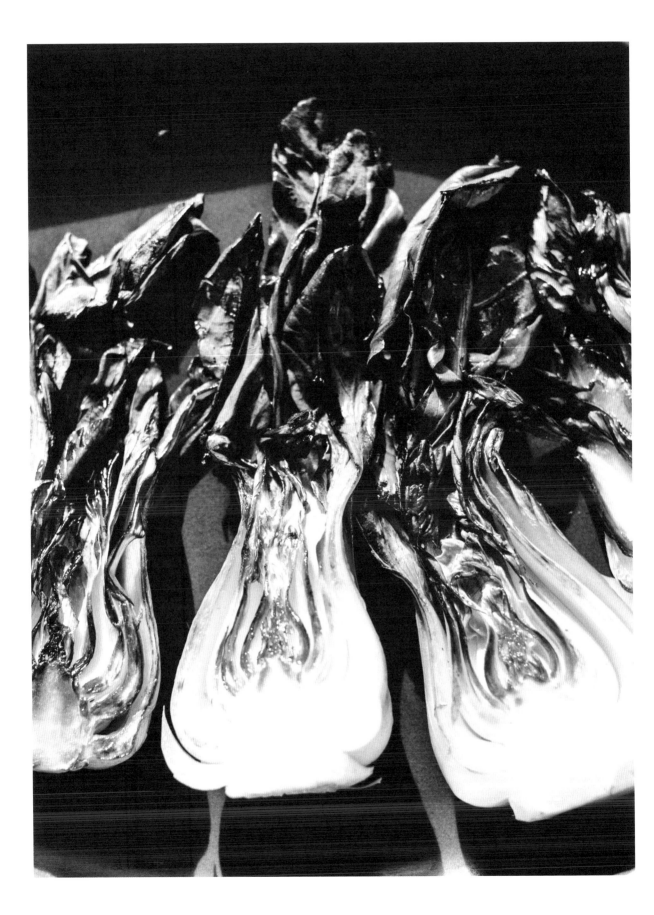

Two ingredients in this recipe—baby bok choy and anchovy—are, in my opinion, not used nearly enough in kitchens. Anchovy butter with grilled meats is one of my go-tos when I have guests over, and people who don't think they like anchovy usually change their minds. Buy a high-quality anchovy and you won't end up with an overpowering fishy flavor.

SEARED BOK CHOY

INGREDIENTS

4 baby bok choy

Grapeseed oil

2 tablespoons Anchovy Butter (below)

Water

PROCEDURE

Heat a stainless-steel pan to medium-high heat with just enough grapeseed oil to lightly cover the bottom of the pan. Cut each bok choy in half lengthwise and set the halves in the pan cut-side down. Sear until golden brown, about 5 minutes. Flip the bok choy and add 2 tablespoons anchovy butter. Turn the heat to medium low and add 1 tablespoon of water. Let the butter and water emulsify without separating and baste the bok choy for about 1 minute with the butter. Remove from heat and set aside.

ANCHOVY BUTTER

INGREDIENTS

1 cup butter, softened

1 tablespoon drained and rinsed capers, minced

1 clove garlic, minced

1 teaspoon lemon zest

⅓ cup chopped parsley

1 teaspoon kosher salt

2 small anchovy filets

PROCEDURE

Whip all ingredients together in a stand mixer fitted with the paddle attachment until thoroughly combined.

TO FINISH

Plate two nice slices of steak with two of the bok choy halves and drizzle the plate with some butter from the pan. Finish the steaks with a small dollop of butter and let it melt. Sprinkle with a bit of salt if desired after the steaks are cut.

Roasted Tenderloin
with warm bacon and spinach salad

>>>———→ · ←———<<<

Turns out spinach *does* taste good when mixed with a healthy dose of bacon and
mustard. Even Popeye would approve. The trick to this salad is to only partially wilt the
spinach by pouring the hot bacon vinaigrette over it and then trapping the heat in the
mixing bowl by covering it with plastic wrap or placing the pan used to cook the bacon
over the bowl. Depending on how fatty the bacon is, the amount of dressing you get
can vary. Start by pouring what appears to be a good amount of dressing to match the
amount of spinach, and then add more if necessary. It's easier to add more dressing than
to remove it.

ROASTED TENDERLOIN

INGREDIENTS

Grapeseed oil

1½ pounds venison tenderloin

Kosher salt

PROCEDURE

Heat a cast-iron pan over high heat. Add enough grapeseed oil to coat the bottom of the pan. Season the tenderloin with salt and place it in the pan. Turn the heat down to medium high and sear the loin on all sides until it's evenly browned and cooked to an internal temperature of 130°F (54°C). Remove the loin and set it aside to rest for 5 to 7 minutes.

WARM BACON AND SPINACH SALAD

INGREDIENTS

1½ pounds baby spinach

4 strips bacon, chopped

1 shallot, finely minced

2 tablespoons Dijon mustard

2 tablespoons red wine vinegar

¼ teaspoon kosher salt

½ teaspoon ground black pepper

PROCEDURE

Place the spinach in a large metal mixing bowl and set aside. In a sauté pan over medium heat, render the chopped bacon. When the bacon starts to develop color and is getting crisp, whisk in the shallot, mustard, vinegar, salt, and pepper. Sauté until the shallots soften, about 5 minutes, then pour the hot dressing over the spinach. Cover the bowl with the cooking pan until the spinach has slightly wilted, about 1 or 2 minutes. Toss the salad to evenly coat the spinach and add more dressing if necessary.

TO FINISH

Slice the tenderloin into ¼-inch slices and shingle them on a plate. Place a bit of the salad next to the loin and drizzle a little bit of any remaining vinaigrette over the sliced loin.

BUTTER-POACHED TENDERLOIN
WITH SAUCE GRIBICHE AND SEARED ZUCCHINI

Butter-poaching is an extravagant way to finish the cooking process on any meat—especially venison. It turns each bite into a melt-in-your-mouth moment that won't soon be forgotten. This recipe works well with leg steaks or tenderloins. You want to keep the muscle in a larger chunk (about 10 to 16 ounces), give it a good sear in a hot cast-iron pan, and let it soak in a butter bath that's resting at about 135 to 140°F (57 to 60°C), which will slowly finish cooking the meat. This is a great way to cook a bunch of steaks at once because if your butter is the right temperature, it will be very hard to overcook the steaks.

If the butter bath is directly over the top of a flame, make sure to use a small resting rack in the pan so the steaks are not resting directly on the bottom, which will cause them to overcook. If there's no way to make that system work, create a double boiler to warm the butter. Place two like-sized pans on top of each other; the bottom one should contain water, and the top one should hold the butter. Place that over a burner to melt the butter.

The zucchini here uses a technique similar to the Caramelized Cabbage on page 167. Get a rimmed baking sheet wicked hot in the oven and drop thick-cut zucchini slices onto it to give them a nice sear.

BUTTER-POACHED TENDERLOIN

INGREDIENTS

2–4 pounds butter, melted

2 (10-ounce) venison tenderloin steaks

Kosher salt

Ground black pepper

Grapeseed oil

PROCEDURE

First get your butter bath ready. Get it into a place where it will maintain a steady temperature of 135 to 140°F (57 to 60°C), and make sure that you have enough butter in the pan so the loins will fit into it and be covered.

Season your steaks with salt and pepper and set them aside. Heat a sauté pan over high heat, and when it just starts to smoke, add a coating of grapeseed oil to the pan. Turn the pan down to a medium-high heat and gently place the steaks into the pan. Sear on all sides and remove. Place the meat in the butter and let it rest in there for about 45 minutes, or until it reaches an internal temperature of 130°F (54°C).

> I do my double boilers by covering a 4-inch, ⅓-size pan with the same-sized pan and placing them over a low flame. Any same-sized, non-glass meatloaf pans will work. After the meat is out of the butter, save the butter and chill it for use next time.

SAUCE GRIBICHE

INGREDIENTS

½ teaspoon kosher salt

1 tablespoon Dijon mustard

1 tablespoon champagne vinegar

3 tablespoons grapeseed oil

1 tablespoon capers

2 cornichons, finely chopped

1 hard-boiled egg, finely chopped

Ground black pepper

1 tablespoon chopped parsley

PROCEDURE

In a medium mixing bowl, whisk together the salt, mustard, vinegar, and oil, then stir in the capers, cornichons, and egg. Add salt and pepper to taste. Immediately before serving, add the chopped parsley.

SEARED ZUCCHINI

INGREDIENTS

3 medium zucchini

2 tablespoons grapeseed oil

Kosher salt to taste

Ground black pepper to taste

PROCEDURE

Place a rimmed baking sheet large enough to hold the zucchini in a 450°F (232°C) oven. Cut the zucchini into ½-inch-thick rounds, then toss them in a large mixing bowl with oil, salt, and pepper. When the baking sheet is hot, remove it from the oven, carefully lay the zucchini rounds on the sheet, and place it back into the oven. Cook for about 7 minutes, or until the slices are brown (but not black) and still have some crunch to them.

TOMATO-AND-BROWN-SUGAR-BRAISED SHOULDER
WITH WHITE CHEDDAR AND JALAPEÑO GRITS

This is a fairly easy braise that packs a ton of flavor. It's sweet, savory, and has a nice hit of acidity. Cooking the venison at a low temperature very slowly is the key—a slow cook will help it stay tender. When making the grits, try to get them to a consistency of good oatmeal—too thin and they don't mop up the braise, too thick and they're not pleasant to eat.

BRAISED SHOULDER

INGREDIENTS

4 pounds venison picnic shoulder

Grapeseed oil

½ cup champagne vinegar

Kosher salt

2 tablespoons butter

1 yellow onion, diced

2 cloves garlic, thinly sliced

¼ cup packed brown sugar

2 teaspoons ground black pepper

2 teaspoons ground cumin

1 teaspoon smoked paprika

1 (28-ounce) can diced fire-roasted tomatoes

1 cup Bone Broth (see page 56) or chicken stock

PROCEDURE

Dice the picnic shoulder into ½-inch cubes, but don't worry about being too accurate with this dice as it will begin to crumble a bit after cooking. Heat a large soup pot over high heat, and when it's hot, add enough grapeseed oil to just cover the bottom of the pan. Add the venison to the pot in a single layer spread evenly across the bottom of the pan. (Success key: Do not stir the venison—you want it to start to develop deep colors on one side, and stirring will prevent this.) Turn the heat down to medium high and let the meat begin to brown, making sure it doesn't burn in any one spot, which might require moving the pan around on the burner to accommodate for higher and lower temperature zones. During the cooking process, the meat will release a certain amount of moisture; let that cook off, and then you'll notice the browning start to begin. Once there's a solid, even brown layer on the bottom of the pan, add the champagne vinegar and a good pinch of salt and, with the help of the liquid, scrape up all of the brown bits until the bottom of the pan looks clean. Immediately turn down the heat until it's at a very low simmer and reduce the vinegar until it's 80 percent evaporated, about 10 minutes. Remove the meat and set it aside. Add the butter, onion, and garlic to the pan and sauté until the onion is just turning translucent, about 5 minutes. Add the meat, brown sugar, pepper, cumin, paprika, tomatoes with their juices, and bone broth. Bring to a simmer. Let simmer until the venison begins to soften, about 1½ to 2 hours. (Success key: Slow and low is the key here—simmering too aggressively will dry out the already lean protein.)

WHITE CHEDDAR AND JALAPEÑO GRITS

INGREDIENTS

3 tablespoons butter

1 yellow onion, diced

1 jalapeño, diced

7 cups Bone Broth (see page 56) or chicken stock

1 cup ground grits

2 teaspoons kosher salt

½ teaspoon ground black pepper

1 cup grated sharp cheddar cheese

½ cup whole milk

PROCEDURE

In a stockpot, melt the butter over medium-high heat, then add the onion and jalapeño. Let them cook together until the onion is translucent, about 5 minutes. Add the bone broth and bring it to a boil. Slowly whisk in the grits until they are fully incorporated. Turn the heat down until the grits are at a gentle simmer. Stir occasionally until the grits are fully cooked, about 45 minutes. Stir in the salt, pepper, cheese, and milk and add more stock if necessary.

TO FINISH

Place a large spoonful of grits in the bottom of a bowl and indent the pile with the back of a spoon. Add a large scoop of the braised venison with plenty of sauce into the indent.

SHOULDER STEAK CONFIT
WITH CARAMELIZED CABBAGE, MEAT SAUCE, AND CHAMPAGNE VINAIGRETTE

Getting nice eating steaks out of a shoulder can be challenging due to all the connective tissue in that area, but this slow-cooking technique turns a muscle full of fat and gristle into a succulent, mouth-watering steak. Right above the scapula toward the neck there's a good-sized cut that works well for this recipe, but any same-sized steaks from that area will do. The dry rub really penetrates the meat to make a very flavorful steak.

The trick to getting the caramelized cabbage right is heating up a rimmed baking sheet in the oven before the cabbage goes on it. You'll really get some nice crispy bits that way, similar to the zucchini in page 161.

The Meat Sauce and Champagne Vinaigrette found on pages 151 and 80, respectively, make excellent accompaniments.

SHOULDER STEAK

INGREDIENTS

1 tablespoon kosher salt

1 tablespoon ground black pepper

1 tablespoon ground fennel

1 pound venison shoulder, cut into 4 steaks (about 1 inch thick each)

1 pound rendered pork lard

½ lemon, sliced

5 sprigs fresh oregano

5 sprigs fresh thyme

PROCEDURE

In a small bowl, combine the salt, pepper, and fennel to make the rub. Evenly season each steak with the rub, spreading the seasoning equally over the steaks. Transfer the steaks to a plate, cover with plastic wrap, and refrigerate for 4 hours. In a stovetop-safe baking dish that will fit all the steaks in one layer, melt the lard over low heat on the stovetop. Once the lard is melted, place the steaks into the baking dish and surround them with the lemon slices and herbs. Adjust the heat as needed to make the lard just barely simmer. Continue to cook for the steaks for about 3 hours or until the steaks are just beginning to fall apart. Low temperatures are very important here or the steaks will dry out.

When ready to serve, pull the steaks from oil using a fish spatula and let them drip off any excess oil before plating.

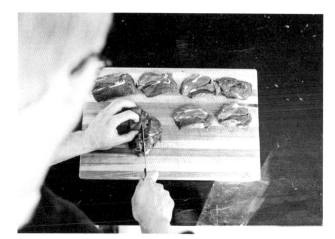

CARAMELIZED CABBAGE

INGREDIENTS

1 small red cabbage, cored, quartered, and thinly sliced

4 tablespoons grapeseed oil, divided

2 teaspoons kosher salt

PROCEDURE

In a large mixing bowl, mix the cabbage, 2 tablespoons grapeseed oil, and salt. Preheat your oven to 500°F (260°C) and place 2 rimmed baking sheets in the oven for 8 to 10 minutes, or until they're hot. Take them out and place 1 tablespoon grapeseed oil on each one. Working quickly, place the cabbage on the hot baking sheets in a single layer and put them back in the oven as quickly as possible. Let the cabbage cook for 6 minutes, then open the oven and give the cabbage a quick stir, mixing the browned bits on the edges into the less-cooked middle areas. Close the oven door and let the cabbage cook for another 5 minutes, or until its starts to get brown and crisp with no blackened areas.

TO FINISH

Toss the hot cabbage with enough champagne vinaigrette to evenly coat the cabbage but not so it's swimming in vinaigrette. Lay a pile of the cabbage on a plate and place the steak directly on top. Top with a large spoonful of meat sauce.

WHOLE CONFIT DEER LEG
WITH GRILLED FLATBREAD, FRUIT COMPOTE, COMPOUND BUTTER, AND PESTO

This is a tough, ballsy, all-in recipe, and you have to be dedicated to make it happen. I've only done it once to date, but the end result was one of the best meals I've ever made—and we fed somewhere in the vicinity of twenty people. It's one that I plan on doing over and over in the future when the time is right.

This recipe is based off a traditional duck confit, but it's made with an entire venison leg cooked in a large pan of animal fat. To get enough rendered fat for this, pork fat will most likely be your best bet, but if for some reason you happen to have enough duck fat lying around, please call me up and I will immediately come eat dinner at your home.

You will want a pan that's large enough to fit an entire deer leg from the shin up as well as all the melted fat on top of it. I used a thick-walled, deep hotel pan that you can find at a local restaurant store for about $20. Due to the fact that there's absolutely no way to eat this with fewer than ten people, have your guests bring the accoutrements that go along with it. I liked it best on grilled flatbreads with an assortment of pickles, spicy garnishes, fermented vegetables, sweet and savory sauces, and fresh vinaigrettes. If you're extra ambitious, the flatbread, pesto, and compote are three good accompaniments.

WHOLE CONFIT DEER LEG

INGREDIENTS

1 venison hindquarter

1 cup kosher salt

½ cup ground black pepper

¼ cup ground coriander seeds

2 tablespoons ground juniper berries

Rendered pork fat, enough to cover the leg

½ lemon, sliced

5 sprigs fresh oregano

5 sprigs fresh thyme

PROCEDURE

Mix the salt, black pepper, and dried spices in a mixing bowl. Evenly coat the venison leg with the mixture, rubbing them into the meat as you work. Wrap the leg tightly in plastic wrap and place it back into the refrigerator for 48 hours. After the 48 hours, remove the leg from the refrigerator and place it into a large cooking vessel. In a separate soup pot, warm the rendered pork fat to a liquid stage, but not boiling. Place the lemon, oregano, and thyme in the vessel with the venison leg and pour the pork fat over the top of the leg until it's just submerged. If you're cooking the leg stovetop, place the vessel on top of a burner on very low heat, so it's barely bubbling, for 3½–4 hours or until the meat just begins to fall off the bone. If you'd like to cook it in the oven, heat the oven to 275°F (135°C), cover the pan with a lid, and let the leg cook for 4–4½ hours or until the meat just begins to fall off of the bone. Once the meat is cooked, remove the pan from the oven or stovetop and let it cool for 45 minutes before handling.

FLATBREAD

INGREDIENTS

1 package active dry yeast (about 2¼ teaspoons)

1 teaspoon sugar

1 teaspoon kosher salt

¾ cup warm (but not hot!) water

2 cups all-purpose flour

Grapeseed oil

PROCEDURE

Mix the yeast, sugar, salt, and warm water in a large mixing bowl. Let it sit until the yeast begins to activate and you see some foam forming, roughly 15 minutes. Add the flour and mix until the dough is combined evenly. Let the dough rise for 1 hour or so, until it's doubled in size. While the dough is rising, get your grill ready to use at a medium-hot temperature. On a floured surface, knead the dough until there are no more lumps. Cut the dough into 4 portions and roll them out until they're about ¼ inch thick. Brush one side of the dough with grapeseed oil and throw it on the grill. While it's grilling, brush the other side with grapeseed oil. Once the grilling side begins to brown, flip it and cook the other side. When that side is brown, remove it from the grill.

FRUIT COMPOTE

INGREDIENTS

½ cup dried cranberries

¼ cup dried currants

1 cup chopped apple (use a tart variety)

Zest of half a lemon

2 teaspoons champagne vinegar

½ teaspoon chopped fresh sage

¼ teaspoon chopped fresh rosemary

1 teaspoon honey

½ cup water

PROCEDURE

In a heavy-bottomed saucepan over medium-low heat, combine all the ingredients and bring them to a simmer. Reduce the heat to low and continue to cook the mixture until it thickens and the fruits begin to break down, stirring occasionally. Cook for about 30 minutes or until it has a jam-like consistency.

PESTO

INGREDIENTS

1 cup fresh basil

1 cup fresh parsley

2 tablespoons toasted walnuts

2 cloves garlic

Juice of half a lemon

½ cup grapeseed oil

½ cup freshly grated Parmesan cheese

PROCEDURE

Using a food processor fitted with a steel blade, combine the basil, parsley, walnuts, garlic, and lemon juice until the herbs and nuts are finely minced. Slowly stream in the oil while the machine is running, and run until the pesto becomes emulsified. Add the Parmesan and refrigerate until ready to serve.

TO FINISH

Carefully remove the deer leg from the oil and place on a large platter. Serve condiments and flatbread on the side with spoons and let your guests pig out!

INDEX

A

Anchovy Butter, 157

B

backstrap, 32, 33
Bacon Brussels, 92
Bacon Jam, 69
barbecue sauce, 63
beans, 54–55, 136
Biscuits with Country-Style Venison Sausage
    Gravy, 95
Black and Blue Gut Loin Carpaccio, 74–75
Blackened Sirloin, 132–137
Blistered Green Beans, 136
Bone Broth, 56
Bourbon-Maple Butter, 129
breads, 60, 169
breakdown, 32–39
Breakfast Sausage with Over-Easy Eggs and
    Bacon Brussels, 91–94
broth, 56
Burgers with Sweet Potato Fries and
    Chimichurri, 115–118
butchery, 22, 32
Butter-Poached Tenderloin, 160–161

C

Caramelized Cabbage, 167
Cast-Iron–Seared Venison, 59–61
Cauliflower Purée, 144
Champagne Vinaigrette, 80
cheeses
    Creamy Blue Cheese, 73
    Seasoned Ricotta, 79
    White Cheddar and Jalapeño Grits, 163

Cherry Barbecue Sauce, 63
Chile Honey Mustard Dressing, 60
Chili, Venison and Pineapple, 86–87
Chilled Asparagus Salad, 79
Chimichurri, 118
Coleslaw, 112
Cori's Hot Dish, 131
Creamy Blue Cheese, 73
Creamy Kale, 106

D

deer hunting, 9, 14
deer populations, 9
deer processing
    breakdown, 32–39
    field dressing, 24–27
    sectioning, 40–43
    skinning, 28–31
dressings
    Champagne Vinaigrette, 80
    Chile Honey Mustard Dressing, 60
    Garlic , Anchovy, and Herb Vinaigrette, 110
    Herb Vinaigrette, 137

E

eggs, 94
Ember-Roasted Root Vegetables, 129
ethics, 14

F

Farro and Brussels Sprouts Soup with Venison
    Leg, 81
Fennel Cabbage Slaw, 122
field dressing, 24–27
Flatbread, 169

forequarters
  breakdown, 34, 36
  sectioning, 37, 40
Fruit Compote, 169
Fry Bread, 60

G

Garlic , Anchovy, and Herb Vinaigrette, 110
Garlic Aioli, 75
Garlic, Ginger, and Chile Oil, 53
gravy, 95
Gremolata, 56
Grilled Lemons, 107
Grits, White Cheddar and Jalapeño, 163
gut loins, 32
gutting, 24–27

H

Heart Skewers, 50–53
Herb Vinaigrette, 137
hindquarters
  breakdown, 35, 39, 40
  sectioning, 43
hunters, 9, 14

J

Jalapeño Poppers, 66

L

Leg Sandwiches, 71–73
Leg Skewers, 54–55
Lettuce Wraps, 65
liver, 24
loin sections, 32
Lomo El Trapo, 152–157

M

Mashed Potatoes, 148
meals, 19, 46
Meat Sauce, 151
Meatballs with Cherry Barbecue Sauce, 62–63
Meatloaf, 126–129
middles
  breakdown, 34, 36
  sectioning, 42
Molasses Braised Shoulder, 66

N

neck, 84

O

Over-Easy Eggs, 94

P

Pan-Seared Loin, 141–144
Pesto, 169
pickles, 61
Pico de Gallo, 122
Porcini-Encrusted Loin, 147–151
potatoes. see vegetables

R

Raw Kale Salad with Leg Paillard, 110
recipe tips, 19, 46
Rib Rub, 72
ribs, 42
Roasted Shoulder, Seasoned Ricotta, and
    Chilled Asparagus Salad, 76–80
Roasted Tenderloin, 158–159

S

salads
  Chilled Asparagus Salad, 79
  Raw Kale Salad with Leg Paillard, 110
  Warm Bacon and Spinach Salad, 159
Sauce Gribiche, 161
sauces
  Cherry Barbecue Sauce, 63
  Meat Sauce, 151
  Pesto, 169
  Sauce Gribiche, 161
Sausage Braise with Sauerkraut and Bone
    Broth, 99
Schnitzel with Creamy Kale and Charred
    Lemons, 100–107
Seared Bok Choy, 157
Seared Zucchini, 161
Seasoned Ricotta, 79
sections, 40–43
shanks, 43
Shoulder Steak Confit, 165–167
skinning, 28–31
Smoked Leg Steak with Coleslaw, 112
soups
  Farro and Brussels Sprouts Soup, 81
  Venison Neck Split Pea Soup, 84
spreads
  Anchovy Butter, 157
  Bacon Jam, 69
  Bourbon-Maple Butter, 129
  Creamy Blue Cheese, 73
  Garlic Aioli, 75
Stovetop Beans, 55
Sweet Potato Fries, 118

T

Tacos, 121–122
Tenderloin Carpaccio, 74
Terrine, 68–69

Toasted Breadcrumbs, 144
Tomato-and-Brown-Sugar–Braised Shoulder,
    162–163
trophy hunting, 9

V

vegetables. see also beans; salads
  Bacon Brussels, 92
  Caramelized Cabbage, 167
  Cauliflower Purée, 144
  Coleslaw, 112
  Creamy Kale, 106
  Ember-Roasted Root Vegetables, 129
  Fennel Cabbage Slaw, 122
  Mashed Potatoes, 148
  Seared Bok Choy, 157
  Seared Zucchini, 161
  Sweet Potato Fries, 118
  Whole Roasted Cauliflower, 144
  Winter Pickles, 61
Venison and Pineapple Chili, 86–87
Venison Neck Split Pea Soup, 84
Venison Paillard, 111
Venison Sausage Gravy, 95
vinaigrettes. see dressings

W

Warm Bacon and Spinach Salad, 159
White Cheddar and Jalapeño Grits, 163
whitetail deer, 9
Whole Confit Deer Leg, 168–169
Whole Roasted Cauliflower, 144
windpipe, 24
Winter Pickles, 61

ABOUT THE AUTHOR

Educated at the New York City's French Culinary Institute, **Jon Wipfli** left behind the world of high-end commercial kitchens to form Slay to Gourmet and The Minnesota Spoon, businesses that cater private events and teach small classes in whole-hog butchery and technique-based cooking. Jon lives in Minneapolis.

ACKNOWLEDGMENTS

Thanks to Scott and Barb for providing me with the tools to be an outdoorsman and to Joe, Nick, Ben, Tyler, and Sam for always wanting to hunt. Thanks to Matt for making things look good, the *Growler* magazine for giving me a space to write about hunting, and Dennis at Voyageur Press for thinking it was cool. This book wouldn't exist without all of your help.